THE GOSPEL OF PHILIP

THE GOSPEL OF PHILIP

JESUS, MARY MAGDALENE,
AND THE GNOSIS
OF SACRED UNION

Translation from the Coptic
and commentary by
JEAN-YVES LELOUP

English translation by
JOSEPH ROWE

Inner Traditions
Rochester, Vermont

Inner Traditions
One Park Street
Rochester, Vermont 05767
www.InnerTraditions.com

LIBRARY OF CONGRESS CATALOGING-IN-PUBLICATION DATA

Evangile de Philippe. English & Coptic.
    The gospel of Philip : Jesus, Mary Magdalene, and the gnosis of sacred union / Coptic translation and commentary by Jean-Yves Leloup ; English translation by Joseph Rowe ; foreword by Jacob Needleman.—1st U.S. ed.
        p. cm.
    ISBN 1-59477-022-0 (pbk.)
    1. Gospel of Philip—Commentaries. 2. Gnosticism. I. Leloup, Jean-Yves. II. Rowe, Joseph, 1942– III. Title.

2004110340

Printed and bound in the United States at Lake Book Manufacturing

10   9   8   7   6   5   4   3   2

Text design and layout by Priscilla Baker
This book was typeset in Caslon with Copperplate Gothic as the display typeface

CONTENTS

LIST OF ABBREVIATIONS

1 Cor	First Epistle of Paul to the Corinthians
Acts	Acts of the Apostles
Jer	Book of Jeremiah
John	Gospel of John
Luke	Gospel of Luke
Mark	Gospel of Mark
Matthew	Gospel of Matthew
Philip	Gospel of Philip
Thomas	Gospel of Thomas*

---

* [Included in James M. Robinson, ed., *The Nag Hammadi Library in English, Translated and Introduced by Members of the Coptic Gnostic Library Project of the Institute for Antiquity and Christianity,* 4th rev. ed. (Leiden: E. J. Brill, 1996) — *Ed.*]

FOREWORD

The discovery in 1945 of manuscripts that have come to be known as the Gnostic gospels was one of the most momentous archaeological finds of our time. Accidentally unearthed by an Egyptian peasant near the desert village of Nag Hammadi and dating from the very beginnings of the Christian era, these texts have exerted a profound influence on our thinking about the origins and nature of Christianity, an influence that continues to grow with every passing year.

Like many of these "Gnostic" documents, the text of the Gospel of Philip consists mainly of sayings and doctrines attributed to Jesus—here called Yeshua*—which point to an astonishing body of knowledge about man and the cosmic world and about the practices leading to inner freedom and the power to love. As is common in all the great spiritual traditions of the world, this knowledge is expressed mainly in allegory, myth, and symbol, rather than in the intellectual language we have become accustomed to in science and philosophy.

How are we modern men and women to understand these ancient sayings and symbols? What are they telling us about the illusions that suffocate our minds and freeze our hearts—and about the way of life that can actually awaken us to what we are meant to be? Do these texts ask us to deny essential doctrines of Christianity that throughout the ages have brought hope to millions? Many observers view them in that way. For

---

* "Jesus" in Aramaic, and in Hebrew, *Yehoshua*.

others, the effect of these documents has been to provoke a hardened skepticism that dismisses them with such labels as "superstition," or "heresy." Yet another widespread reaction has been to treat this material as justification for either uncritical speculation about the life and mind of Jesus or blanket condemnation of those who sought to stabilize the institution of the Church in the turbulent centuries immediately following the death of Jesus.

The work of Jean-Yves Leloup presents a wholly different approach to these writings, one that is formed by a rare combination of spiritual questioning and masterful erudition. As has already been shown in his translation and study *The Gospel of Mary Magdalene*, these "Gnostic" codices must be offered to us in a way that helps us to hear them—to hear what they actually may be saying in response to our era's newly awakened need. It is as though after two thousand years of Abrahamic religion—Judaism, Christianity, Islam—the unending barbaric violence and moral desolation of humankind has finally brought the whole of our global world to a life-or-death hunger for a new kind of knowing and moral direction.

Can the ideas and practical indications contained in the Gospel of Philip and the other Nag Hammadi texts be approached as something more than fascinating curiosities far from the so-called mainstream of our culture's canons of knowledge and faith? Is the world itself, or enough people in the world who can make a difference, ready to hear with new ears the forgotten wisdom of humankind offered in a language free of the opinions and emotional associations that have decayed into illusory certainties and eviscerated moral sensibilities?

Perhaps such texts as the Gospel of Philip contain, necessarily in the form of symbolic language, a treasury of *answers* that we as individuals might have all but given up hope of finding. In a time when the role of religion in human life has become one of our world's most agonizing concerns, texts such as the Gnostic gospels invite us to risk stepping back in a new way from many of our most cherished opinions not only about the teaching and acts of Jesus, but about who and what we are as human beings. As this book indicates, it is in this specific new effort of separating from our own thoughts and feelings that an entirely unexpected source of hope may be glimpsed, both for ourselves and for our world.

To begin to understand this text, we need to have a question, and to question ourselves. That said, the issue then becomes not only what are our questions, but *how* do we ask them? What does it really mean to have a serious question of the heart and to ask it from the whole of ourselves, or at least from the part of ourselves that is able to hear an answer? For one of the most remarkable aspects of spiritual knowledge (in the ancient meaning of the term *gnosis*) is that its answers can be fully received only in response to a real question, a real need. And it is no doubt true—and also often forgotten—that the inner meaning of all scripture, whether canonical or not, can be received only in the state of spiritual need. If approached without this need or genuine state of questioning, texts such as the Gospel of Philip are likely to be either regarded at arm's length as mere scholarly and archaeological riddles or curiosities, or greedily appropriated as fuel for fantasy. The first step then toward a new kind of questioning, a new kind of knowing, is a step back into ourselves, apart from all that we think we know about ourselves. If there is such a thing as transformational knowing (and this is the true meaning of the term *gnosis*), its first stage is the inner act of *not knowing*.

In his beautiful and courageous introduction to the Gospel of Philip, Jean-Yves Leloup concludes by saying, "I have articulated some of the questions raised by this gospel. I have never pretended to have the answers to these questions . . ." Yet he goes on to add that "this must not lead me to deny the nearness of a source that is capable of satisfying the thirst for these answers."

He does not dare to name that "source." But as we turn the pages of the text itself, we may begin to sense numerous indications of its nature in the bittersweet state of self-questioning that this gospel can evoke. Under Jean-Yves Leloup's hand, we are guided to both the known and the unknown in ourselves and in our understanding of the Christian teaching.

Concerning our relationship to the teachings of Christianity, Leloup invites us to regard this hitherto "hidden" and "secret" text as pointing to the hidden or *subconscious* teachings of Christianity, in the sense that what is ontologically subconscious in human life is what secretly influences and directs that which we call our consciousness. This is to be contrasted with the well-known or, in this limited sense of the word, conscious canonical Gospels under the light of which, in Leloup's words, the Church originally "staked a claim, so to speak, on the entire territory of Christianity, fencing in a land that was originally open and free."

We might also think of the subconscious and the conscious as *essence* and *manifestation*—what we are in the depths of our hidden being and how we act and manifest in the conditioned and relative realm of time and the world we live in. It might also be suggested that in our own individual lives, as well as in the life of a great tradition that compassionately struggles to penetrate the worldly life of humankind, essence and manifestation often drift apart from each other, to the point that outer expression or manifestation loses or "forgets" its source and essence—and thereby, knowingly or unknowingly, even contradicts or denies the authority of its source. In that case, to confront essence and manifestation together, especially in their accrued mutual contradiction, is nothing less than a great shock of awakening—and it is there where we may experience the state of self-questioning that is both joyous and bittersweet.

In this sense, speaking in terms of *gnosis* or sacred knowing, a genuine question that corresponds to a state of spiritual need involves the experience in ourselves of our own essential being together with our actual manifestation. It means being present to both the divine essence within and how we manifest or act in ways that generally serve only the illusions and attachments of the ego. There can be great suffering in this awareness of how we forget or betray the truth of what we are. But this awareness itself, when it is deep enough, opens the way to a reconciliation of these two opposing currents in ourselves, and this awareness can lead us toward "the peace that passes understanding." Here knowledge and love fuse.

Jean-Yves Leloup's inspired approach to the Gospel of Philip is articulated in the opening pages of his introduction: "It is not my intention," he writes, "to set the canonical and the apocryphal gospels against each other, nor privilege one over the others. My aim is to read them together: to hold the manifest together with the hidden, the allowed with the forbidden, the conscious with the unconscious." The reconciling force of such an honest approach to this text, which open-heartedly examines subversive ideas with patience, humility, and respect, allows us to *hear* the way Yeshua speaks of the meaning of sacramental bread and wine; of the *true* and *"illusory"* human body; of the meaning of death and resurrection as stages on the path of inner work; of the purity of the Virgin as the immaculate and fertile silence *(parthenos)* or void within the human soul; or—in what is bound to attract much attention—in the way Jesus is allowed to speak about marriage and sexuality. There is a teaching here that is very deep and very high, and woe to us if we too hastily attach ourselves to one or another surface meaning of what is expressed in these pages. The text speaks of the sexual act in marriage as "the holy of holies," and Jean-Yves Leloup offers wise and heartfelt reflections about the possible sexuality of Jesus himself in his fully realized humanness. At the same time we find such passages as the following:

> *Even the worldly embrace is a mystery;*
> *Far more so, the embrace that incarnates the hidden union.*
> *It is not only a reality of the flesh,*
> *For there is silence in this embrace.*
> *It does not arise from impulse or desire* [epithumia]*;*
> *It is an act of will.*
> *It is not of darkness, it is of light.* (Page 84, Plate 130)

At this point we may recall the oft-repeated warning of Jesus in both the canonical and apocryphal gospels: "Let those who have ears to hear, hear." For at the very least, what seems to be spoken of here is the meaning of sexuality in its highly evolved, fully human form. Who among us is yet able to claim enduring access to such a quality of the fully human?

Even on the purely theoretical or theological plane, Leloup's approach to this apocryphal material can produce entirely new currents of energy and understanding in our approach to the teachings and person of Jesus. The relevance of these texts is meant to go beyond their impact on our understanding of Christianity as a religion existing outside of ourselves. But what exactly *is* their relevance to our own personal lives now and here—to ourselves as we are and try to be?

Christian or not, we are all children of our era and we have heard that Truth is for all who seek it—whether in Christian terms, in the language of any of the other great spiritual traditions, or in the language of a new, authentic revelation of spiritual knowledge; whether through the sacredness of nature as science reveals it to us, or simply through people, individual men and women whose presence radiates the light of hope in the darkening night of our world.

Nearly every page of this translation can evoke intense self-questioning, offering directions of personal search for Truth that are as profound as they are startlingly new and challenging. The words of Jesus stand to meet us there: "Seek and ye shall find." Perhaps, then, the one real question we all can share and ponder is not *whether* to seek, but *how* to seek, how to discover and accept our own real need. I can think of no better platform from which to approach this powerful text and its fertile commentary.

JACOB NEEDLEMAN,
DEPARTMENT OF PHILOSOPHY,
SAN FRANCISCO STATE UNIVERSITY, AND AUTHOR OF
LOST CHRISTIANITY AND *THE AMERICAN SOUL*

INTRODUCTION

THE INVENTION OF THE GOSPELS

When the cross upon which Christ was supposedly crucified was discovered by Empress Helena in Jerusalem, the phrase *invention of the cross* was used. In Latin *in venire* means "to be brought to light," "to emerge." The original meaning of *invention* is a coming to light of what is already there—it is both a discovery and a return.

In this sense, we might speak today of an *invention of the Gospels*, meaning those that were already there but lay in oblivion for many centuries, buried in the sands near Nag Hammadi in Upper Egypt. Might this rediscovery of forgotten Gospels, beginning in 1945, also be an "invention of Christianity"? Might it be an occasion for a return to the sources of a tradition that is thought to have been aware of its own roots, but which in reality has been largely ignorant of them?

Some would detect here a "return of the repressed": These sacred texts and inspired writings express and reveal the collective unconscious of a people or group. Thus these rejected Gospels reappearing in our time would be manifestations of a return of Christianity's repressed material.

They are often called *apocryphal*, meaning "hidden" or "secret." The original Greek word, as evidenced in the prefix *apo-*, means "under"—"underneath" the scriptures.

Similarly, that which we call *unconscious* or *subconscious* refers to what is underneath consciousness—and may secretly influence or direct this so-

1

called consciousness. In this sense we might also speak of these as "unconscious Gospels"—for their language is in fact closer to that of dreams than of history and reason, which we have come to associate with the so-called canonical Gospels. The latter were put to effective use in building Church institutions that staked a claim, so to speak, on the entire territory of Christianity, fencing in a land that was originally open and free.

It is not my intention to set the canonical and the apocryphal Gospels against each other, nor to privilege one over the others. My aim is to read them together: to hold the manifest together with the hidden, the allowed with the forbidden, the conscious with the unconscious.

It is interesting that the Church of Rome's current official list of approved biblical scriptures was established only in the sixteenth century at the Council of Trent. It was not until the eighteenth century that Ludovico Muratori discovered a Latin document in Milan containing a list of books that had been considered acceptable to the Church of Rome much earlier, around 180 C.E. Now known as the Muratori Canon, it represents a consensus of that period as to which books were considered canonical (from the Greek *kanon,* a word originally meaning "reed" and then "ruler," or "rule").

Thus the canonical Gospels are those that conform to the rule, and the apocryphal Gospels are those judged not to conform to it. The function of this rule is obviously to establish or maintain the power of those who made it. This was not a process that happened overnight. A significant feature of the Muratori Canon is that it allowed usage of the Apocalypse of Peter, which was later excluded from the Roman canon. Other Gospels, such as the Gospel of Peter, were considered canonical by some Syrian churches until sometime in the third century.

There are those who are disturbed by this indeterminacy in the origins of Christianity. Yet the coming to light of these ancient apocryphal writings, on the contrary, should remind us of the richness and freedom of those origins. If becoming a truly adult human being means taking responsibility for the unconsciousness, which presides over most of our conscious actions, then perhaps now is the time for Christianity to become truly adult. It now has the opportunity to welcome these Gospels, thereby welcoming into consciousness that which has been repressed by our culture. Our culture now has a chance to integrate, alongside its historical, rational, more or less "masculine" values, those other dimensions that are more mystical, imaginary, imaginal[1] . . . in a word, feminine, always virginal, always fertile. The figure of Miriam of Magdala, so often misunderstood and misused, now begins to reveal the full scope of her archetypal dimension.

These Gospels were discovered by Egyptian fellahin less than forty miles north of Luxor, on the south bank of the Nile, in the area of Nag Hammadi at the foot of the Jabal-at-Tarif, in the vicinity of the ancient monastic community of Khenoboskion. It was there that some of the earliest monastic communities of St. Pachomius's order were founded. This collection of manuscripts must have been buried sometime during the fourth century C.E. Thus it was apparently a group of orthodox monks who saved these texts, suspected of being heretical, from destruction.

We must bear in mind the context of theological, and especially Christological, crises that tormented the Christianity of this era. These monks may have buried these priceless texts in order to protect them from the inquisition by the Monophysite hierarchy, which claimed that Christ has only one nature: the divine. His humanity, the hierarchy said, was only a passive instrument used by the divinity. In contrast to this, orthodoxy maintained that Jesus Christ was both truly God and truly human—meaning he was a fully human being, with a sexual body, a soul, and a spirit *(soma, psyche, nous)*. His intimacy with Miriam of Magdala was evidence of this fullness.[2]

---

1. [The word *imaginal,* coined by the philosopher Henry Corbin, refers to an act of creative imagination that transcends the subjectivity of ordinary imagination. See *The Gospel of Mary Magdalene* by Jean-Yves Leloup (Rochester, Vt.: Inner Traditions, 2001); and *The Voyage and the Messenger* by Henry Corbin (Berkeley, Calif.: North Atlantic Books, 1998). —*Trans.*]

2. Cf. Jean-Yves Leloup, *The Gospel of Mary Magdalene* (Rochester, Vt.: Inner Traditions, 2002); and *L'Évangile de Thomas* (Paris: Albin Michel, 1986).

May it have been that these texts were threatened not only by elements of the orthodoxy, as has often been claimed, but also by the Monophysites, who were shocked by certain details evoking the incarnation of the Word with a realism that was too explicit for them? This human body that spoke and taught was also a body that loved—and not merely with a chaste platonic love, but with all the sensual and psychic presence of a biblical love.

THE GOSPEL OF PHILIP

Most of the books of the Nag Hammadi codices are Coptic translations of Greek originals. The Gospel of Philip is a part of Codex II, the most voluminous manuscript in the library of Khenoboskion. The papyrus measures roughly 11 inches long and between 5.5 and 6 inches wide; and the text is 8.5 inches by 5 inches. Each of its 150 pages contains from 33 to 37 lines, whereas the other manuscripts have no more than 26 lines per page. In addition to the Gospel of Philip, Codex II contains the Gospel of Thomas, a version of the Apocryphon of John, the Hypostasis of the Archons, an anonymous writing known as "The Untitled Text" (and sometimes as "The Origin of the World"), the Exegesis on the Soul, and the Book of Thomas the Contender.

The Gospel of Philip was inserted between the Gospel of Thomas and the Hypostasis of the Archons. A photographic edition of Codex II was published by Pahor Labib,[3] with the Gospel of Philip appearing on plates 99–134. A first translation was made by H. M. Schenke,[4] who divided the Gospel into twenty-seven paragraphs. Although this division has been debated (E. Segelberg, R. M. Grant, J. E. Ménard), I have found it useful for this edition. It presents the Gospel of Philip as a kind of garland of words no less enigmatic than those of the Gospel of

---

3. Cf. volume 1 (1956) of the Coptic Gnostic Papyri in the Coptic Museum at Old Cairo.
4. H. M. Schenke, *Koptish-Gnostische Schriften aus den Papyrus Codies von Nag Hammadi* (Hamburg Bergstadt, Theologische Forschung 20, 1960), 33–65; 81–82.

Thomas, and more elaborate, because they are certainly of a later date than the text of Thomas. Several other translations of this Gospel have appeared in German and in English (R. M. Wilson, R.-C. J. de Catanzaro, W. C. Till, Wesley Isenberg). To my knowledge, the only previous French translation is that of my colleague Jacques Ménard, of the University of Strasbourg.[5]

Opinions are divided as to the dating of this Gospel. Giversen and Leipoldt date it to as late as the fourth century. This is unlikely, for it would mean that it disappeared only a few years after it was written. Furthermore, fragments of this text are quoted in previous writings before the third century. I follow Puech's more authoritative dating of approximately 250 C.E. If it is true, as most scholars believe, that this Coptic version is a translation of an earlier Greek text, then it would push back the dating of the original to around 150 C.E. This Gospel poses the same problem as that of Thomas: Being a compilation of passages, we have no means of assigning *all* of these logia to a single date. We must deal with the fact that the evangelic flavor of certain passages contrasts with others (no doubt of later date) that have a more gnostic character. This is not to assign a lesser value to these later passages, for age alone does not confer an automatic certificate of authenticity or orthodoxy. Like all texts considered to be "inspired," the Gospel of Philip is witness to the diverse influences in which the cultures and beliefs of an era mingle. Such diversity always informs the supposedly perennial sources of inspiration.

In this presentation I have followed Professor Jacques Ménard's arrangement of Codex II (indicated by the page number at the top of each page of Coptic text), plus that of Dr. Pahor Labib's photographic edition (indicated by the plate number at the top of each page of Coptic text).

---

5. Jacques Ménard, *L'Évangile de Philippe* (Paris: Édition Cariscrip, 1988). Although our translation and our interpretation are quite divergent from his, our debt to Ménard's overall work remains considerable.

The arrangement of the passages in this translation follows that of H. M. Schenke. I have also found it useful to employ a special numbering of the passages from 1 to 127 to facilitate references to logia.

It would be hard to overemphasize the difficulties involved in the translation from the Coptic of these often sibylline texts. Professor Ménard drove himself to the point of risking his physical and mental health while working on them. I often diverge from him in both translation and interpretation of certain passages, for my concern has always been to find a meaning in these logia, even if it sometimes requires a departure from philological literalism. An archaeologist is required only to make an inventory of the broken fragments of the vase; but the hermeneutist must at least imagine, if not establish, how the vase was used.

There have been a number of more or less serious presentations of these puzzling texts. But when we have been used to laboring within the confines of archaeological and philological reductionism, who would be so bold as to attempt to elucidate their meaning to discover how they might be a source of inspiration for contemporary readers, just as they were for readers of the early centuries of Christianity? The problem with all texts bearing the name Gospel is that we no longer listen to them as Gospels—that is, as good news, as liberating teachings for human beings of all times. Instead we read them as historical documents, curious dead words of the past that are of interest primarily to scholars. Above all, we must seek to find an alive and enlivening meaning in them, as in all inspired scriptures.

With more honesty than modesty, I must admit that the translation presented here falls into the category of an essay rather than a definitive version. I hope that skilled and patient researchers will find it useful in future efforts with this text.

I have learned that to translate is always to interpret. This is where the "passion" of a text lies. The text is *subject* to our interpretation, and is itself a kind of decoding that always involves the subjectivity of a Logos that has been heard, or perhaps only thought. We still do not know what Yeshua really said. We know only what a number of hearers and witnesses have heard. Scripture consists of what has been heard, not what has been said.

PHILIP

Like the Jews in their diaspora, the Christian Jews (or Judeo-Christians) made great efforts to conserve their threatened traditions by putting them into writing. These texts often claimed to have the stamp of authority of one or another of the primary evangelists from Israel and its diaspora: Peter, James, John, Philip, and so forth.

In the ancient world, the concept of literary property was radically different from what it is now. An author who wrote under the name of an apostle was considered to be performing an act of homage, not an act of forgery. *Pseudepigrapha,* the technical term now used to describe this process, was commonly practiced. The Gospel of Philip is pseudepigraphic in this sense, like most of the other Gospels.

Why was the patronage of Philip evoked for this collection of rather long and mysterious writings? In Greek, the name Philip means "lover of horses." In ancient times, the horse was often a symbol of noble lineage, as well as of freedom.

In the canonical Gospels the name Philip is cited on several occasions:

The next day [after the baptism of Yeshua in the Jordan], John the Baptist was still there with two of his disciples. Seeing Yeshua pass, he said: "This is the Lamb of God." Andrew and John heard him and went to Yeshua. Seeing that they were following him, Yeshua turned around, saying: "What do you seek?" They answered: "Master, where are you staying?" He said to them, "Come and see." They went to see, and stayed with him.

The next day Yeshua wished to return to Galilee. He met Philip and told him: "Follow me." Philip was from Bethsaida, the city of Andrew and Peter.

Meeting Nathaniel, Philip said to him, "We have found the one written about by Moses in the Law, and by the prophets; he is Yeshua, the son of Joseph of Nazareth." Nathaniel answered him: "What good can come out of Nazareth?" Philip told him: "Come and see."[6]

Philip, a disciple of John the Baptist, was thus the third to be called by Yeshua, and quickly became a disciple. He used the same words that Yeshua had used in speaking to Andrew and John: *come, leave,* and *see— look, contemplate, discover.*

Philip subsequently takes his place on the list of twelve apostles called by Yeshua. According to Matthew 10:3 and Luke 6:14, he is named as the fifth, just after John. Mark 3:18 lists him after Andrew. In the Acts of the Apostles, after the departure of Judas Iscariot, Philip is named as the fifth among the eleven, just before Thomas. Yeshua seems to have "tested" his faith before accepting him, just prior to the multiplication of the loaves and fishes:

Lifting up his eyes, Yeshua saw a large crowd approaching him, and said to Philip: "Where will we buy enough bread to feed all these people?" He said this to test him, for he knew well what he was going to do. Philip [speaking as a knowledgeable man] replied: "Two hundred dinarii would not buy enough bread for each person to have a little of it."[7]

Shortly before the Passion, as John later recounts, Yeshua had already gone to Jerusalem, and was visibly close to Philip:

Among those who came up to worship during the feast were several Greeks. They came to Philip [his Greek name would have facilitated this], who was from Bethsaida in Galilee, and asked him: "Sir, we wish to see Yeshua." Philip went to tell Andrew, and they both went to tell Yeshua. Yeshua said to them: "The hour has come for the Son of Man to be glorified."[8]

---

6. John 1:35–39; 43–46.
7. Ibid., 6:5–7.
8. Ibid., 12:20–23.

Later, during the conversation between Yeshua and his friends at the Passover meal, Philip is again prominent:

> "If you knew me, you would also know my Father. But henceforth, you will know him, and you have seen him!" Philip said to him: "Lord, show us the Father, that will suffice us." And Yeshua answered him: "I have been with you this long, Philip, and you still do not know me? Whoever sees me, sees the Father. How can you say, 'Show us the Father'? Do you not know that I am in the Father and that the Father is in me? . . . Believe me: I am in the Father, and the Father is in me."[9]

Philip has been called to contemplate, like Thomas, "the One who is before his eyes." He is called to discover his Teacher and, through him, every human being, as a Temple of the Spirit, the abode of the Father. The river cannot exist without its Source. It is by plunging into the river that one can know the Source, which is God. Although "none has ever seen Him," all that exists is witness to God's existence. None has ever directly contemplated the Source of life, yet the smallest act of love and creation is witness to his presence. It is by living that one discovers life. It is the Son in us who knows the Father; the Father of Yeshua is also our Father. Like John, Philip is invited to become the evangelist, or the messenger of the incarnation.

Philip also appears in the Acts of the Apostles. The Teacher had led him to discover the presence of the Principle (the Father) in all its manifestation (the Son); now he has progressed to the point of understanding, from reading the scriptures himself, that Yeshua is the hoped-for Messiah. This is what he teaches the Ethiopian whom he meets on his way:

> However, an angel of the Lord addressed Philip, saying: "Arise, and go south, on the road which goes down from Jerusalem to Gaza, in the desert." Philip arose and left. Then he saw an Ethiopian eunuch, a

---

9. Ibid., 14:7–11.

minister and guardian of the treasure of Queen Candace of Ethiopia, who had come to Jerusalem to worship in the presence of YHWH.

Returning home, he was seated in his chariot, reading the prophet Isaiah.

Then the Spirit said to Philip: "Go forward, and join him in his chariot." Philip approached, and heard that he was reading from the prophet Isaiah. He asked the man: "Do you truly understand what you are reading?"

"How could I, without someone to guide me?" the man answered. And he invited Philip to come up and sit with him.

Now the passage which he was reading was this one:

> *"Like a sheep he was led to the slaughter,*
> *and like a lamb silent before its shearer,*
> *so he does not open his mouth.*
> *In his humiliation justice was denied him.*
> *Who can describe his generation?*
> *For his life is taken away from the earth."*

The eunuch asked Philip, "About whom, may I ask you, does the prophet say this, about himself or about someone else?" Then Philip began to speak, and starting with this scripture, he proclaimed to him the good news about Yeshua. As they were going along the road, they came to some water; and the eunuch said, "Look, here is water! What is to prevent me from being baptized?" He commanded the chariot to stop, and both of them, Philip and the eunuch, went down into the water, and Philip baptized him. When they came up out of the water, the Spirit of the Lord took Philip away; the eunuch saw him no more, and went on his way rejoicing. But Philip found himself at Azotus, and as he was passing through the region, he proclaimed the good news to all the towns until he came to Caesarea.[10]

---

10. Acts 8:26–40.

Here, Philip appears as scriptural hermeneutist, and as baptist. Both of these qualities recur in the Gospel that bears his name. It is also interesting that the person whom he teaches is an Ethiopian royal official. Can it be mere coincidence that it is in Ethiopia that we find, even today, richly ornamented crosses with a representation in the center of a man and a woman joined closely together? For this is one of the most important themes of the Gospel of Philip: the union of man and woman as revelation of the Love of the creator and savior.

Philip is also the apostle of Samaria, where his teaching was accompanied by signs and wonders rivaling those of Simon Magus.

> Philip went down to the city of Samaria and began proclaiming Christ to them. The crowds with one accord were giving attention to what was said by Philip, as they heard and saw the signs that he was performing. For in the case of many who had unclean spirits, they were coming out of them shouting with a loud voice; and many who had been paralyzed and lame were healed. So there was much rejoicing in that city.
>
> Now there was a man named Simon, who formerly was practicing magic in the city and astonishing the people of Samaria, claiming to be someone great; and they all, from smallest to greatest, were giving attention to him, saying, "This man is what is called the Great Power of God." And they were giving him attention because he had for a long time astonished them with his magic arts.
>
> But when they put their faith in Philip preaching the good news about the kingdom of God and the name of Jesus Christ, they were being baptized, men and women alike. Even Simon himself believed; and after being baptized, he did not leave Philip, amazed as he was by the great miracles that he saw taking place.[11]

Philip also appears as a greatly venerated figure in the so-called apocryphal texts. The Pistis Sophia reminds us that "Philip is the

---

11. Ibid., 8: 5–13.

scribe of all the speeches that Jesus made, and of all that he did."

According to historians, all that we can be sure of is that Philip probably preached in Syria and in Phrygia, around the Black Sea, and that he was probably martyred or crucified in Hieropolis. In his ecclesiastical history, Eusebius of Caesarea (V, XXIV) quotes a letter from Polycratus, bishop of Ephesus, to Pope Victor (pope between 189 and 198):

> Great luminaries lie buried with their fathers in Asia, sleeping the sleep of death. They will arise on the day of the coming of the Lord, the day when he comes amidst the glory of the heavens, when he awakens all the saints; Philip, one of the twelve emissaries, lies with his fathers in Hieropolis, and with two of his daughters.

THE MAJOR THEMES OF THE GOSPEL OF PHILIP

What interest is there in translating and studying these often obscure and suppressed texts of the origins of Christianity? First, there is their historical significance. A minimum of honesty demands that we endeavor to know where we come from, what are our sources and our points of reference.

What are the sources and founding texts of the established denominations, of Christianity, of our civilization itself?[12] Christianity is a religion that is little known, if not unknown altogether, and this applies especially to its origins. What we know about it is mostly the history of its institutional churches and their great achievements, but also of their wars, Crusades, and sometimes their obscurantism and their inquisitions.

To reach into Christian origins is to find ourselves in a space of free-

---

12. A historical study of Christianity's origins and founding texts would make a passionately interesting ecumenical project in which Orthodox, Catholic, Protestant, and other churches could bring together their knowledge and skills in a common work.

dom without dogmatism, a space of awe before the Event that was manifested in the person, the deeds, and the words of the Teacher from Galilee. There is an awe and a freedom in interpreting these deeds and words as a force of evolution, transformation, and Awakening for everyone, as well as for those who believe in him.

From an anthropological[13] point of view, these Gospels remind us of the importance of the *nous*, that fine point of the psyche which is capable of silence and contemplation, as mentioned in the Gospel of Mary Magdalene. They also remind us of the importance of the imagination.

In his book *Figures du pensable* (Figures of the Thinkable), Cornelius Castoriadis points out that it is imagination that really distinguishes humans from other animals. As we now know, the latter are capable of thought, calculation, language, and memory; but "human beings are defined above all, not by their reason, but by their capacity of imagination."[14] Imagination is at the deepest root of what it means to be human: Our societies, institutions, moral and political norms, philosophies, works of art, and also what is now called science—all of these are born of imagination.

This recognition of imagination gives rise to a momentous idea: Human beings and their societies can change. For Castoriadis it was the ancient Greeks who first realized the imaginary nature of the great meanings that structure social life. From this realization arose the science of politics—in this sense, the questioning of existing institutions, and changing them through purposive collective action. It also gave birth to philosophy—in this sense, the questioning of established meanings and representations, and changing these through the reflective activity of thought. To politics and philosophy we should add poetry and spirituality, in the sense of their questioning of reality supported only by sensory

---

13. [The author uses the word *anthropology* (Fr. *anthropologie*) in a special way: He means it in its original, pre-modern sense of a comprehensive philosophy of human nature and its place in the cosmos, not as the study of human cultures and biological evolution. — *Trans.*]

14. Cornelius Castoriadis, *Figures du pensable* (Paris: Le Seuil, 1999).

experience and reason to the exclusion of intuition and feeling—in other words, the objective world stripped of a Subject who perceives it or, more exactly, who interprets it and tells its story. There is neither human story nor cosmic story without the presence of imagination to speak it.

When this faculty of imagination is not kept alive, there is no more story to be told, and institutions begin to stiffen and become dogmatic. Their objectifications then take on the quality of absolutes. When imagination becomes stuck or frozen, creation and poetry are no longer possible, and this also closes the door to democratic processes as well the arts and sciences. If people lack imagination, how can they find solutions to the challenges of life?

Thus one of the functions of these inspired texts is to stimulate our imagination—or, more precisely, our power of interpretation. If, as Sartre said, human beings are condemned to be free, then it is because they are condemned to interpret. Neither in the world nor in books do we find anything with a built-in meaning. It is up to human beings to give things meaning and thereby participate in the creative act.

The Gospel of Philip affords us an opportunity for reflection, imagination, and meditation regarding certain aspects of Christianity that are sometimes hidden. The hermeneutic stimulation of this recently discovered text has at times been too strong for some, resulting in excessive and self-indulgent interpretations. For this reason, I have thought it wiser to return this Gospel to its context, and to relate it to the traditions that are its source: the Judaic tradition and the earliest forms of Christianity that grew out of it. This "orthodox" reading is quite distinct from other interpretations that have so far been offered by major commentators. It differs notably from that of my colleague Jacques Ménard, who attempted to make this text fit into the narrow category of Gnosticism, in particular Valentinian Gnosticism. Of course I do not deny such a gnostic influence—the text's numerous terms influenced by the Syriac language testify to it, and we know that this cultural milieu was the matrix of the related currents of Mandaean and Manichean beliefs.

The themes proposed by this garland, or pearl necklace, as I have described this Gospel, are numerous. Like the individual pearls in a strand, each logion shines in its own way and could inspire a long commentary. In the framework of a shorter book, we are limited to only a few of them that seem particularly potent as invitations to deeper questioning and as challenges to certain habitual and preconceived notions.

We recall Peter's question in the Gospel of Mary Magdalene:

> How is it possible that the Teacher talked
> in this manner, with a woman,
> about secrets of which we ourselves are ignorant?
> Must we change our customs,
> and listen to this woman?[15]

Such a question also applies to certain logia of the Gospel of Philip. Must we change our habitual ways of looking at conception, birth, and relations between man and woman? Must we reconsider our entire image of the Christ, of the real nature of his humanity and his relation to women, especially to Miriam of Magdala?

Is sexuality a sin, a natural process, or a space of divine epiphany, a "holy of holies"? These are all themes for which we shall sketch out interpretations here, placing them in resonance with Jewish tradition. But we must also consider other themes that are no less important and just as inspiring for reflection. In logion 21, for example:

> Those who say that the Lord first died,
> and then was resurrected, are wrong;
> for he was first resurrected, and then died.
> If someone has not first been resurrected, they can only die.
> If they have already been resurrected, they are alive, as God is Alive.

---

15. Cf. Jean-Yves Leloup, *The Gospel of Mary Magdalene* (Rochester, Vt.: Inner Traditions, 2002), 157–65.

This reminds us that Resurrection (Anastasis in Greek) is not some sort of reanimation. As the apostle Paul pointedly mentioned in his letter to the Corinthians: "Flesh and blood cannot inherit the Kingdom of God."[16]

The Gospel of Philip invites us to follow Christ by awakening in this life to that in us which does not die, to what St. John called eternal Life. This Life is not "life after death," but the dimension of eternity that abides in our mortal life. We are called to awaken to this Life before we die, just as Christ did.

The apostle Paul further points out that it is not our biological-psychic body that resurrects, but our spiritual body, or *pneuma* in Greek.[17]

What is this so-called spiritual body? Is it not already woven in this life, from our acts of generosity and the giving of ourselves? For the only thing that death cannot take from us is what we have given away. The Gospel of Philip emphasizes this power of giving, this capacity of offering that the *soter* (Greek for "savior") has come to liberate in us. It is this "body given in offering" that is our body of glory, our resurrected being.

It was not only at the moment of his manifestation

that he made an offering of his life,

but since the beginning of the world that he gave his life in offering.

In the hour of his desire,

He came to deliver this offering held captive.

It had been imprisoned by those who steal life for themselves.

---

16. 1 Cor 15:50.

17. Cf. 1 Cor 15 on the subject of resurrection. [It is important to note that the author uses the words *soul* and *spirit* based their original meanings, which are significantly different from their modern usages. In antiquity the Greek *psyche*, which means soul, did not have the same elevated status that the soul assumed in later Christianity, nor was it confused with spirit (*pneuma* in Greek), as it later came to be and still is in current usage. For the ancients the soul included aspects of the mortal body, mind, and emotions, as well as something of the spirit transcending them. It was an *intermediary* reality between the physical and the spiritual. In a further refinement of this intermediation, the *nous* appears here as that "fine point" of *psyche* (soul) that is closest to *pneuma* (spirit).—*Trans.*

He revealed the powers of the Gift
and brought goodness to the heart of the wicked.[18]

As in the other Gospels, we find this metaphysics of the Gift, or *agapē*, which resides in the very heart of Being, and which the Teacher unveils through his words and his acts.

Another important theme showing a kinship between this Gospel and that of Thomas is the idea of non-duality. Some have found a distinctly Eastern flavor in this logion:

Light and darkness, life and death, right and left, are brothers
and sisters. They are inseparable.
This is why goodness is not always good,
violence not always violent, life not always enlivening,
death not always deadly.[19]

Such words offer a challenge to many forms of education and conditioning, but also to political attitudes. In politics it is surely unwise to separate good and evil by too sharp a division: One never occurs without the other, like day and night. This also recalls the parable of the good seed and the unwanted seed in chapter 13 of Matthew: To root out one is also to destroy the other.

Instead, we must wait for the time of harvest, meaning the time of insight. We would so much like to be pure and perfect, mistaking ourselves for God, who alone knows the ultimate meaning of good and evil. Might this be the original mistake, the original pretense or self-inflation, the cause of all kinds of suffering, of hasty judgments and exclusions? Was not Christ himself rejected and crucified by people who considered themselves just?

The Gospel of Philip reminds us of that humility, which is liberating.

---

18. Philip, logion 9:5–11.
19. Ibid., logion 10:1–5.

It is sometimes in the name of the good that the greatest evil is done, and the bloodiest and most unjust crimes are committed in the name of God and his justice. To face this fact should deliver us from fanaticism. We must accept the truth that even the best actions are never performed without at least some bad consequences. It is from the same pollen that the bee produces both honey and venom. Both the saint and (unfortunately) the inquisitor quote the same Gospel passage.

As long as we use words, we will have evils, according to the Gospel of Philip:

> The words we give to earthly realities engender illusion, they turn the heart away from the Real to the unreal. The one who hears the word God does not perceive the Real, but an illusion or an image of the Real.

The same holds true for the words Father, Son, Holy Spirit, Life, Light, Resurrection, Church, and all the rest. These words do not speak Reality; we will understand this on the day when we experience the Real.

> All the words we hear in this world only deceive us.
> If they were in the Temple Space [*Aeon*], they would keep silent
> and no longer refer to worldly things,
> in the Temple Space [*Aeon*] they fall silent.[20]

This silence is that of the apophatic, contemplative theology that continued to develop in the following centuries:

> Of God, it is impossible to say what he is in Himself, and it is more proper to speak of God by denying everything. Indeed, he is nothing that exists. This is not to say that he cannot be in some sense, but that he is above everything that is, above being itself.[21]

---

20. Ibid., logion 11:1–11.
21. Cf. Saint John Damascene, *An Exposition of the Orthodox Faith*, I, 4.

In his *Apologia*, II, St. Justin (100–165 C.E.) says that the terms Father, God, Creator, and Lord were not divine names, but names for the blessings and works of the divine.

Though it is good to be silent, it is still necessary to speak. Here, too, the Gospel of Philip avoids the trap of "either/or" dualism:

> The Truth makes use of words in the world
> because without these words, it would remain totally unknowable.
> The Truth is one and many,
> so as to teach us the innumerable One of Love.[22]

We are in the world, and this world is one of words and misunderstandings. We must nevertheless try to make ourselves heard, if not understood. This is what the Gospel of Philip invites us to do in dealing with subjects that were undoubtedly the source of much misunderstanding in his times, as they still are today.

THE SACRED EMBRACE, CONCEPTION, AND BIRTH

Without trust and consciousness in the embrace, there is nothing "sacred." There is only release, desire-fulfillment, and biological well-being. Procreation is possible, but not creative engendering and conception. This theme in Philip has roots in the Jewish tradition and is developed quite explicitly in the later writings of the Kabbalah.

In kabbalistic literature, the manner of procreation is emphasized as being an essential link between a society and its ultimate destiny. Body and mind are equally involved in the act, to the point that the "spark" of divinity is said to implant itself in the matter of engendered bodies via the

---

22. Philip, logion 12:7–10.

movement of thought of the parents during their moment of union. It is as if this thought had in itself the power to incarnate—to employ a word overly rich in implications—the divine in the heart of engendered bodies, and thus to perpetuate a genealogical lineage of altogether extraordinary quality.[23]

The Gospel of Philip distinguishes birth from conception. Some children are well born but poorly conceived; conception is linked with imagination and desire, with an encounter between two beings, not merely two appetites. This is why logion 112 claims:

> A woman's children resemble the man she loves.
> When it is her husband, they resemble the husband.
> When it is her lover, they resemble the lover.

It is possible to procreate children (through impulse and chance) without having conceived them; and they can be conceived in different ways. There are troubled or impure conceptions (i.e., the result of egocentricity or selfish aims). There are also immaculate conceptions, with pure intentions (i.e., giving freely, an expression of creative generosity, a child desired for itself).

There is also a decisive role played by desire, imagination, and the thoughts of the parents regarding their future child as a member of a *holy people* in either the inner or the outer sense of that term. An intimate relation founds an intimate genealogy, which ultimately depends on intention and desire more than on any historical or juridical status.[24]

Compare the above with the following passage from the beginning of logion 30 of the Gospel of Philip:

> "All those who are begotten in the world

---

23. Cf. Charles Mopsik, translation and commentaries, *Lettre sur la sainteté. Le secret de la relation entre l'homme et la femme dans la cabale, étude préliminaire* (Paris: Verdier, 1986), 16–17.
24. Ibid., 15–16.

are begotten by physical means;

the others are begotten by spiritual means."

Again, the resonance between this Gospel and the later Jewish tradition is striking. The physical act of love harbors a secret that has serious implications for the whole problem of a "chosen" or "holy" people, or a Kingdom of God. And the question of our possible membership in such an elect turns out to have nothing to do with the family or ethnicity to which we belong. Instead, it has to do with the quality of trust and consciousness in the embrace, which makes us children of the nuptial act, icons of the union.

In the thirteenth-century *Letter on Holiness*, attributed to Rabbi Moses ben Nahman,[25] this theme recurs:

The *Letter on Holiness*, or *Iggeret ha-Kodesh*, is only one of several titles by which this work has been known. No doubt it is the most widely-known, but surely the most evocative of these titles is *The Secret of Sexual Relations*. This shows the real subject matter of the letter, but his main concern is to bring holiness—divine life—into the very heart of the intimate act between couples. What is at stake in this concern is very crucial: nothing less than the reproduction of Israel as a "holy people," according to the Biblical expression. How to give birth to children of a holy people, to Jews belonging to the Israelite community, is not a question with an obvious answer. The attempt to answer it must not go astray in a fog of legalistic rules defining inheritance and kinship, such as a Jew being defined as a child born to a certain person, or worse yet, enthno-genetic theories that define Jews as those of certain ancestors, and so forth. We know something about how one becomes a holy person; there exists a whole panoply of rules and disciplines for this. But for

---

25. Also known as Nahmanides (1194–1270), a Spanish rabbi who emigrated to Palestine. [This letter has more recently been attributed to Rabbi Joseph Gikatilla, q.v. later in the introduction. —*Trans.*]

the author of the *Letter on Holiness,* to be born holy, to be born as a member of the people of Israel, requires a special attitude of the parents during the crucial moment that determines the form of the embryo: the sexual act. This holiness cannot be conferred by the mere transfer of hereditary traits. Nor does it have anything to do with the child's status in the social, juridical, or religious order. Education plays no role yet. The entire significance of a "holy" lineage hinges on a voluntary, conscious act of love and spiritual meditation involving the parents—plus a few clinical precautions regarding the act of intimacy. But it is made clear that this intimate transmission of essential Judeity is totally out of the control of any social identity norms. No human tribunal is capable of judging mystical "intentions." In this way, there emerges an Israel-being which eludes any scholarly definition. Consequently, the simple fact of being a Jew partakes of mystery: The secret of being Jewish is how one was conceived, not how one was born.[26]

Instead of the usual moral or clinical point of view, often accompanied by rationalizing or repressive tendencies, the *Letter on Holiness* treats the sexual act as belonging to the divine realm. It accords it the status of an act of theophany, exactly as does the Gospel of Philip. The sacred scriptures that societies have chosen to accept as references have undoubtedly had enormous influences, not only on the history of theology, but also on social behavior and mores—and the rejection of certain other scriptures has had immeasurable consequences.

Charles Mopsik is particularly explicit on this point:

The idea of God that monotheistic religions have imposed upon people seems to exclude any reference to sexuality as a way of approaching or experiencing the divine. Moreover, the concept of the unique God as an all-powerful Father, with no feminine partner, has formed the consen-

---

26. Cf. Charles Mopsik, *Lettre sur la sainteté,* 14–15.

sual basis of ordinary theological discourse. This has deeply influenced Western philosophy and the metaphysics that has grown out of it. These mental frameworks and representations have had all kinds of consequences for Christian and Islamic history and civilization, as well as for Judaism. These ideas have penetrated so deeply into people's minds that they do not realize they are the fruit of a particular religious ideology, and far from axiomatic. The inability of contemporary believers and non-believers to free themselves from these structures is partly due to the fact that these religious and philosophical systems have proclaimed their concept of an asexual or unisexual God as the only reasonable one, and have relegated all others to the category of mythology. They pretend to be the sole inheritors of the biblical tradition, and jurists and theologians of the three monotheistic religions see differing conceptions of divinity as dangerous deviations.[27]

Yet at the origins of Christianity, in the heart of the Jewish communities from which it arose, another voice had made itself heard:

"The mystery which unites two beings is great;
without it, the world would not exist."[28]

That passage from Philip resonates with the biblical tradition: In the beginning, as Genesis says, YHWH created *male and female* in his own image. Hence it is neither man nor woman that is in the image of God, but the relation between them. Philip also resonates with the Western philosophical tradition:

There is a certain age at which human nature is desirous
of procreation—procreation which must be in beauty and not in

---

27. Ibid., 7.
28. Philip, logion 60:2–3.

deformity; and this procreation is the union of man and woman, and is a divine thing.[29]

This may come as a surprise to those who associate Plato with readings that cast suspicion on "the works of the flesh." But we must also point out that equally divergent interpretations have arisen from readings of Genesis.

Some have seen Plato's teaching as an evocation of the androgynous nature of humanity—at once male and female—a kind of primordial wholeness for which we have a nostalgic longing. Erotic love would thus appear to be a desperate yearning for our missing half. In Greek mythology and thought, the separation of man and woman is seen as a punishment. In Hebrew mythology and thought, however, this same separation is seen as a blessing and gift of the Creator (for example, the passage from Genesis, "He saw that it was not good for man to be alone"). Sexual differentiation is even seen as an opportunity to gain deeper knowledge of the creative source of all that lives and breathes.

The goal of a sexual relationship is not merely to regain our missing half, thereby gaining access to individuation, or to our original androgynous nature. That part of ourselves seeks its other half is really a kind of self-love; there is no access to otherness here, only a sort of inward differentiation, which is deemed painful and unfortunate.

In the Hebrew tradition, as in the Gospel of Philip, love is more a seeking of one wholeness for another wholeness. It is born not of lack, of *penia*, but of *pleroma*, an overflowing toward otherness.

A human being is born either male or female, but he or she must become a man or a woman—not just mature biologically, but become a person, a subject capable of meeting another person or subject, in a love that is not needy or demanding. Trust and consciousness in the embrace is the echo of this love.

Here is how we might symbolize the Greek and the Hebrew views:

---

29. Plato, *The Symposium,* translation by Jowett.

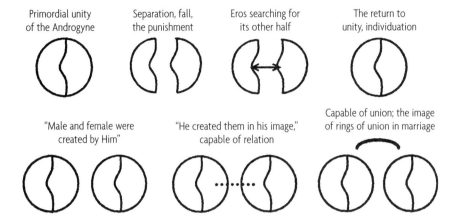

Primordial unity of the Androgyne | Separation, fall, the punishment | Eros searching for its other half | The return to unity, individuation

"Male and female were created by Him" | "He created them in his image," capable of relation | Capable of union; the image of rings of union in marriage

Certain authors of the Hebrew tradition trace this encounter all the way back to two beings who are sexually differentiated but share a single soul, or a single breath, before birth itself. This is a metaphysical way of emphasizing the fact that we were created to form a couple, through which we experience the epiphany of the presence *(shekhina)* of YHWH.

In his book on "the secret of how Bathsheba was destined for David since the six days of the beginning," Rabbi Joseph Gikatila writes:

> And know and believe that at the beginning of the creation of man from a drop of semen, the latter comprises three aspects: his father, his mother, and the Holy Blessed-Be-It. His father and mother shape the form of the body, and the Holy Blessed-Be-It shapes the form of the soul. And when a male is created, his feminine partner is necessarily also created at the same time, because no half-form is ever created from above, only a whole form.[30]

Rabbi Todros ben Joseph HaLevi Abulafia (1222–1298) also said:

30. Rabbi Joseph Gikatila, *Le Secret du mariage de David et Bethsabée* (Paris: Éditions de l'Éclat, 1994), 45–46.

Know that we have in our hands a tradition which says that the first man had two faces *(partsufim)*, as Reb Jeremiah said . . . ; and know clearly that all the parts of the true tradition *(kabalah)*, taken as a whole and in their details, are all built on this foundation. They revolve around this point, for it is a profound secret which mountains depend upon . . . ; according to the initiates of the truth of which the tradition is truth, and of which the Teaching (Torah) is truth, the two verses in question do not contradict each other: *male and female were created by Him;* and *in the image of God he created them* (both from Genesis 1:27). The two verses are one. He who knows the secret of the image, of which it is said: *in our image in our likeness* (Genesis 1:26) will understand. . . . I cannot explain it, for it is not permitted to put this thing in writing, even indirectly, and it is to be transmitted only by word of mouth to upright men, from the faithful to the faithful, and only chapter titles and generalities are to be transmitted, "for the details will tell themselves." These last words are borrowed from the formula of Haguira IIb on the rules for transmission of the secrets of the *Maaseh Merkaba* (Workings of the Chariot), and they are of great interest to us, inasmuch as they clearly show that the masculine/feminine duality is the foundation of the Kabbalists' concept of the divine Chariot. Moreover, the Kabbalah as a whole is considered to be founded on the secret of this dyad. Thus sexual difference characterizes the human soul, the "image" in which it was created, as is the divine realm which is its model.[31]

Thus both in the Jewish tradition and in the Gospel of Philip, the love relationship is not to be used for our own fulfillment, for the relationship itself is our own fulfillment, and the revelation of a third term of love, between lover and beloved. This third term is the source of differentiation as well as of union. The biblical tradition calls it God, and the evangelical tradition calls it *pneuma,* or the Holy Spirit, the breath that unites two beings.

---

31. Quoted in Charles Mopsik, *Lettre sur la sainteté*, 27.

This theme of the union of two breaths turns out to be especially important in the Gospel of Philip.

THE BREATH THAT UNITES: THE KISS OF YESHUA AND MIRIAM

The Teacher loved her [Miriam] more than all the disciples;
he often kissed her on the mouth.[32]

The many reactions aroused by this logion, which I have previously discussed in *The Gospel of Mary Magdalene,* recall a strange state of affairs: Whereas Yeshua has often been depicted with a young man resting his head on his breast (and such images have not been without effect on the behavior of the clergy), it is practically unimaginable to paint him in a pose of intimacy with a woman. It is as if such contact with a woman would detract from the perfection of his humanity and his divinity, though the very opposite is the case. How many times will it be necessary to repeat the adage of the early church Fathers: "That which is not lived is not redeemed"? In other words, that which is not accepted is not transformed?[33]

Was Jesus Christ fully human, a "whole man" (as Pope Leo the Great said, *Totus in suis, totus in nostris*), or not?

The doctrine of the Council of Chalcedony says so: "Christ is at once perfect *(totus)* in his divinity and perfect *(totus)* in his humanity." Thus to depict him as sexually defective should amount to blasphemy. So why all the fuss?

A serious consideration of this subject is required. The Gospels discovered not so long ago at Nag Hammadi invite us to do so. It would undoubtedly help us to be free of the guilt, unhappiness, and degradation that have surrounded what, if one takes the biblical texts seriously, is a

32. Philip, logion 55:3–4.
33. See Jean-Yves Leloup, *The Gospel of Mary Magdalene,* 10–13.

means of knowing and participating in the holiness of God himself.

St. Odilon of Cluny uttered the following words. How was this possible?

> Feminine grace is nothing but blood, humors, and bile . . . and we who recoil at the touch, even with the tips of our fingers, of vomit and excrement, how could we therefore desire to hold in our arms the very sack of excrement itself?

How could anyone desire to canonize such hatred and contempt?

In any event, the Gospel of Philip has Yeshua embracing Miriam on the mouth, and with love rather than disgust. We must emphasize once more that the meaning of this kiss cannot be understood apart from the Judaic and gnostic context of that era.

> You must know in your turn what the ancient ones—blessed be their memory—have taught. Why is the kiss given on the mouth rather than some other place? Any love or delight that aims for true substance can express itself only by a kiss on the mouth, for the mouth serves as source and outlet of the breath, and when a kiss is made on the mouth, one breath unites with another. When breath joins with breath, each fuses with the other, they embrace together, with the result that the two breaths become four, and this is the secret of the four. This is even more true of the inner breaths (the *sefirot*), which are the essence of all; so do not be surprised to find them intertwined in each other, for it expresses their perfect desire and delight.[34]

We must also mention the kiss in the *Song of Songs,* as well as God's kiss to Moses at the moment of his expiring. The Hebrew word for kiss *(nashak)* means "to breathe together; to share the same breath." And the word for breath is the same as the word for spirit; this is true not only in

---

34. *Pirouch esser sefirot belima* (Kabez al Yad: Éditions Scholem, 1976), 372.

Hebrew *(ruakh),* but also in Greek *(pneuma)* and Latin *(spiritus).* Thus Yeshua and Miriam shared the same breath and allowed themselves to be borne by the same spirit. How could it be otherwise?

Charles Mopsik notes that the kiss of union does not necessarily imply a sexual aspect to the relationship, though it may be a prelude to it. It is in this union that the secret is revealed, a secret that leads us to the bridal chamber. For the Gospel of Philip, as for the older Hebrew tradition, this chamber is the holy of holies.

THE BRIDAL CHAMBER, HOLY OF HOLIES

. . . and the holy of holies is the bridal chamber . . .

Trust and consciousness in the embrace are exalted above all.

Those who truly pray to Jerusalem

are to be found only in the holy of holies . . .

the bridal chamber.[35]

This logion only reinforces the resonance between this Gospel and the *Letter on Holiness* attributed to Nahmanides, which offers a kind of explanation:

The sexual relationship is in reality a thing of great elevation when it is appropriate and harmonious. This great secret is the same secret of those cherubim who couple with each other in the image of male and female. And if this act ever had the slightest taint of anything ignoble about it, the Lord of the world would never have ordered us to make these figures, and to place them in the most sacred and secure of places, built upon a very deep foundation. Keep this secret and do not reveal it to anyone unworthy, for here is where you glimpse the secret of the loftiness of an appropriate sexual relationship. . . .

If you understand the secret of the cherubim, and the fact that the

---

35. Philip, logion 76:11–18.

[divine] voice was heard [in their midst], you will know that which our sages, blessed of memory, have declared: In the moment when a man unites with his wife in holiness, the *shekhina* is present between them.[36]

If this is really true, if the union of man and woman is the holy of holies where his presence (*shekhina*, Sophia) is manifest, the place where his breath is communicated *(ruakh, pneuma),* how is it possible for Pope Innocent III (d. 1216) to say, "The sexual act is itself so shameful as to be intrinsically bad," or for one of his theologians to say, "The Holy Spirit departs of itself from the bedrooms of married couples performing the sexual act, even when it is done only for procreative purposes"?

Both Jewish tradition and the Gospel of Philip say exactly the opposite. If any wedding chamber were really abandoned by the Holy Spirit, it could only result in the birth of "animal humans" rather than beings capable of knowledge and worship of God. Hence the place of holiness has become a place of vilification, and the intimation of paradise has been reduced to a gateway to hell.

In his *Meïrat Enayim,* Rabbi Isaac d'Acco offers this parable:

A newborn infant was abandoned in a forest with nothing but grass and water for nourishment. He grew up, and here is what happened to him: He went to a place where people were living and one day saw a man coupling with his wife. At first he laughed at them, saying "So what is this simpleton doing?" Someone told him: "It is thanks to this act, you know, that the world continues. Without it, the world would not exist." The child exclaimed: "How is it possible for such a base and filthy act to be the cause of a world so good, so beautiful, and so praiseworthy as this one?" And they answered: "It is the truth, all the same. Try to understand it."[37]

---

36. Charles Mopsik, *Lettre sur la sainteté,* 231–32.
37. Ibid., 132.

Nahmanides adds: "When the sexual relation points to the name, there is nothing more righteous and more holy than it." Yet it is necessary to "point to the name." For the pure, everything is pure. Purity resides in the intention and motivation that direct the act. This recalls the previously discussed theme of the transmission of holiness as something more than biological genealogy.

> The elders kept their thoughts in the higher realms and thereby attracted the supreme light toward the lower ones. Because of this, things came in abundance and thrived, according to the strength of the thought. And this is the secret of the oil of Elisha, as well as of the handful of flour and the jar of oil of Elijah. It was because of these things that our masters, blessed of memory, said that when a man joins with his wife with his thought anchored in the higher realms, this thought attracts the higher light downward, and this light settles in the very drop [of semen] upon which he is concentrating and meditating, as it was for the jar of oil. This drop thereby finds itself linked always to the dazzling light. This is the secret of: *Before you were formed in the womb, I knew you* (Jer 1:5). This is because the dazzling light was already linked to the drop of this righteous man in the moment of sexual love [between his parents], after the thoughts of this drop had been linked to the higher realms, thus attracting the dazzling light downward. You must understand this fully. You will then grasp a great secret regarding the God of Abraham and Isaac, and Jacob. These fathers' thoughts were never separated from the supreme light, not for an hour or even an instant. They were like servants indentured for life to their lord, and this is why we say: *God of Abraham, God of Isaac, and God of Jacob.*[38]

There are many other texts from the Jewish tradition that could help us to better understand the Gospel of Philip. Moshe Idel, of the Hebrew

---

38. Ibid., 249–50.

University of Jerusalem, has already pointed out the connections between this tradition and Christian gnostic texts.

> It seems certain that these texts reflect a Jewish notion of the pre-existing Temple. In the *Midrash Tanhuma,* regarding the reference to the royal bed in the *Song of Songs,* the anonymous commentator says: "His bed is the Temple. To what here below is the Temple compared? To a bed, which serves to bear fruit and increase. The same applies to the Temple, for everything that was found there bore fruit and was increased." This allows us to conclude that a sexually nuanced perception of the holy of holies already existed in ancient Judaism. Shortly after the destruction of the temple, we find that the bridal chamber substitutes for it as a place where the Shekhina (Presence of God) resides.

The whole exercise *(mitzvah)* proposed by the Teacher in the Gospel of Philip consists of introducing love and consciousness into each of our acts, including the most intimate. In this way, this space-time (the world) becomes a space-temple, a place of manifestation of the presence of YHWH, the One Who Is (*I am who I am,* Exodus 3:14), in complete clarity, innocence, and peace.

In a future work I hope to offer a very detailed analysis of each logion of the Gospel of Philip, relating it to its Jewish, gnostic, and canonical Gospel parallels. For now, I have had to content myself with a translation of this difficult and fascinating text, along with some suggestions for possible interpretations. In this introduction I have articulated some of the questions raised by this Gospel. I have never pretended to have the answers to these questions, yet this must not lead me to deny the nearness of a source that is capable of satisfying the thirst for these answers.

THE GOSPEL
OF PHILIP

[PAGE 53, PLATE 99]

ΟΥϨΕΒΡΑΙΟC P̅ΡΩΜΕ [ΨΑ]ϤΤΑΜΙΕ ϨΕΒΡΑΙ
30 ΟC ΑΥΩ ΨΑΥΜΟΥΤΕ [ΕΡΟ]˳Ϥ˳ ΝΤΕΕΙΜΙΝˏΕˏ
ΧΕ ΠΡΟCΗΛΥΤΟC ΟΥΠ[ΡΟCΗΛ]ΥΤΟC ΔΕ ΜΑϤ
ΤΑΜΙΕ ΠΡΟCΗΛΥΤΟ[C P̅ΡΩΜΕ ΜΜ]ˏΗˏΕ ΜΕ̄
CΕΨΟΟΠ Ν̅ΘΕ ΕΤΟΥˏΨˏ[ΟΟΠ ΧΙΝ ΨΟΡΠ]
ΑΥΩ CΕΤΑΜΕΙΟ Ν̅ϨΝ̅ΚΟˏΟˏ[ΥΕ ΔΕ ΕΥΨΟΟΠ]

[PAGE 53, PLATE 99]

1   A Hebrew who makes someone else a Hebrew is called a
    proselyte.

But a proselyte does not always make other proselytes.

Authentic beings are who they have always been,

and what they engender is authentic:

simply becoming who one is.

[PAGE 54, PLATE 100]

[Ṗ].Ṛ.Ṃ.Ṃ.[ME Ч]ⲢⲰⲮⲈ ⲈⲢⲞⲞⲨ ⲰⲓⲚⲀ ⲈⲨⲚⲀ
ⲰⲰⲠⲈ · Ⲡ[ⲌⲘ].ⲌⲀⲖ. ⲘⲞⲚⲞⲚ ⲈЧⲰⲒⲚⲈ ⲀⲢ̄ Ⲉ
ⲖⲈⲨⲐⲈⲢ.Ⲟ.[Ⲥ] .Ṃ.ⲀЧⲰⲒⲚⲈ ⲆⲈ Ⲛ̄ⲤⲀ ⲦⲞⲨⲤⲒⲀ
Ⲙ̄ⲠⲈЧⲬⲞ[ⲈⲒ]Ⲥ ⲠⲰⲎⲢⲈ ⲆⲈ ⲞⲨ ⲘⲞⲚⲞⲚ ⲬⲈ
5 ЧⲞ Ⲛ̄ⲰⲎⲢⲈ ⲀⲖⲖⲀ ⲦⲔⲖⲎⲢⲞⲚⲞⲘⲈⲒⲀ Ⲙ̄ⲠⲈⲒ
ⲰⲦ ⲰⲀЧⲤⲀⲌⲄ̄ Ⲛ̄ⲤⲰЧ ⲚⲈⲦⲢ̄ⲔⲖⲎⲢⲞⲚⲞⲘⲈⲒ
Ⲛ̄ⲚⲈⲦⲘⲞⲞⲨⲦ’ Ⲛ̄ⲦⲞⲞⲨ ⲌⲰⲞⲨ ⲤⲈⲘⲞⲞⲨⲦ’
ⲀⲨⲰ ⲈⲨⲔⲖⲎⲢⲞⲚⲞⲘⲈⲒ Ⲛ̄ⲚⲈⲦⲘⲞⲞⲨⲦ’ ⲚⲈ
ⲦⲢ̄ⲔⲖⲎⲢⲞⲚⲞⲘⲈⲒ Ⲙ̄ⲠⲈⲦⲞⲚⲌ Ⲛ̄ⲦⲞⲨ ⲤⲈⲞⲚⲌ
10 ⲀⲨⲰ ⲤⲈⲢ̄ⲔⲖⲎⲢⲞⲚⲞⲘⲈⲒ Ⲙ̄ⲠⲈⲦⲞⲚⲌ ⲘⲚ̄ ⲚⲈⲦ
ⲘⲞⲞⲨⲦ ⲚⲈⲦⲘⲞⲞⲨⲦ ⲘⲀⲨⲢ̄ⲔⲖⲎⲢⲞⲚⲞⲘⲈⲒ
Ⲗ̄ⲖⲀⲀⲨ [Ⲡ]ⲰⲤ ⲄⲀⲢ ⲠⲈⲦⲘⲞⲞⲨⲦ ЧⲚⲀⲔⲖⲎⲢⲞⲚⲞ
ⲘⲈⲒ ⲠⲈⲦⲘⲞⲞⲨⲦ ⲈЧⲰⲀⲔⲖⲎⲢⲞⲚⲞⲘⲈⲒ Ⲙ̄
ⲠⲈⲦⲞⲚⲌ ЧⲚⲀⲘⲞⲨ ⲀⲚ ⲀⲖⲖⲀ ⲠⲈⲦⲘⲞⲞⲨⲦ’
15 ЧⲚⲀⲰⲚⲌ Ⲛ̄ⲌⲞⲨⲞ ⲞⲨⲌⲈⲐⲚⲒⲔⲞⲤ Ⲣ̄ⲢⲰ
ⲘⲈ ⲘⲀЧⲘⲞⲨ Ⲙ̄ⲠⲈЧⲰⲚⲌ ⲄⲀⲢ ⲈⲚⲈⲌ ⲌⲒⲚⲀ
ⲈЧⲚⲀⲘⲞⲨ ⲠⲈⲚⲦⲀⲌⲠⲒⲤⲦⲈⲨⲈ ⲈⲦⲘⲈ ⲀЧ’
ⲰⲚⲌ ⲀⲨⲰ ⲠⲀⲒ̈ ЧⲄⲚⲆⲨⲚⲈⲨⲈ ⲈⲘⲞⲨ ЧⲞⲚⲌ
ⲄⲀⲢ ⲬⲒⲘ̄ ⲠⲤⲞⲞⲨ Ⲛ̄ⲦⲀⲠⲬⲤ̄ ⲈⲒ ⲤⲈⲤⲰⲚⲦ̄ Ⲙ̄

[PAGE 54, PLATE 100]

2   The slave desires freedom; the extent of his master's wealth is
of little importance.

The Son, he who is Son, possesses the heritage of the Father.

3   To inherit from the dead is to die, to inherit from the living is
to live.

The Living One gives us birth and death as our heritage.

The dead do not inherit; how could they inherit?

If the dead were to inherit from the living, they would live.

4   Atheists do not die, because they have never lived.

Only those who hold to the truth know what life is.

They may well fear death, because they live!

5   The Presence of Christ creates the new world;

He brings order and beauty among us;

death recedes.

20 ПКОСМОС СЕРКОСМЕІ ЙЙПОЛЕІС СЕ
ЧІ ЙПЕТМООУТ · ЕВОЛ · ЙⲌООУ ΝΕΝ'ШО
ΟΠ ЙⲌΕΒΡΑΙΟС ΝΕΝΟ ЙΟΡΦΑΝΟС ΝΕΥ
ЙΤΑΝ ЙΤЙΜΑΑΥ ЙΤΑΡЙШШΠΕ ΔΕ Й
ΧΡΗСΤΙΑΝΟС ΑΕΙШΤ ⲌΙ ΜΑΑΥ ШШΠΕ ΝΑ

25 ΝΕΤСΙΤΕ ⲌЙ ΤΠΡШ ШΑΥШСⲌ ⲌЙ ΠШШΜ'
ΤΠΡШ ΠΕ ΠΚΟСΜΟС ΠШШΜ' ΠΕ ΠΚΕΑΙ
ШΝ ΜΑΡЙСΙΤΕ ⲌЙ ΠΚΟСΜΟС ΧΕΚΑΑС
ΕΝΝΑШСⲌ ⲌЙ ΠШШΜ · ΔΙΑ ΤΟΥΤΟ ШШΕ
ΕΡΟΝ' ΕΤЙΤΡЙШΛΗΛ · ⲌЙ ΤΠΡШ ΠΙΕΒΟΛ

30 ⲌЙ ΤΠΡШ ΠΕ ΠШШΜ' ΕΡШΑΟΥΑ ΔΕ ШСⲌ
ⲌЙ ΤΕΠΡШ ΕΥ.Ν.ΑШСⲌ ΑΝ ΑΛΛΑ ΕΥΝΑⲌШ
ΛΕ ⲌШС ΠΑ.Τ.[Ο Й].Τ.ΕΕΙΜΕΙΝΕ ΕΥΝΑΤΕΥ
Ε ΚΑΡΠΟ.С. [ϬΕ] ΑΝ' ΟΥ ΜΟΝΟΝ ΕΥЙΝΗΥ
ΕΒ.Ο.[Λ ⲌΜΠΜΑ ΑΝ] .Α.ΛΛΑ ⲌЙ ΠΚΕСΑΒΒΑΤΟΝ

35 [ΤΕΥϬΟΜ ΟΥ]ΑΤΚΑΡΠΟС ΤΕ ΑΠΕΧⲢС ΕΙ

6   When we were Hebrews, we were orphans, knowing only our
    mother; becoming Christians, we discover both our mother
    and our father.

7   Those who sow in winter reap in summer; winter is this world,
    summer is the world of Openness. Let us sow in the world,
    so as to harvest in summer.

    To pray is not to prevent winter, but to allow summer.

    Winter is not a time of harvest, but of labor.

8   Without seeds, the earth bears no fruit;

    indolence is not the Repose and Power of the *Shabbat*.

9   Christ came to deliver some and to save others.

    He made strangers his own;

    in their differences, they manifested his will.

[PAGE 55, PLATE 101]

ϨⲞⲈⲒⲚⲈ ⲘⲈⲚ ⲈⲦⲢⲈϤⲦⲞⲞ[Ⲩ].Ⲥ.[Ⲉ Ϩ].Ⲛ̄.ⲔⲞⲞⲨ.Ⲉ.

ⲆⲈ ⲈⲦⲢⲈϤⲚⲀϨⲘⲞⲨ ϨⲚ̄ⲔⲞⲞ[Ⲩ]Ⲉ ⲈⲦⲢⲈϤⲤⲞ

ⲦⲞⲨ ⲚⲈⲦⲞ Ⲛ̄ϢⲘⲘⲞ Ⲛ̄ⲦⲀϤⲦ.ⲞⲞ.ⲨⲤⲈ ⲀϤⲀ

ⲀⲨ Ⲛ̄ⲚⲈⲦⲈ ⲚⲞⲨϤ ⲚⲈ ⲀⲨⲰ ⲀⲨⲚⲞⲨϨ.Ⲉ.

5 Ⲛ̄Ⲛ̄ⲈⲦⲈ ⲚⲞⲨϤ', ⲚⲀⲈⲒ Ⲛ̄ⲦⲀϤⲔⲀⲀⲨ Ⲛ̄ⲚⲈⲞⲨ

Ⲱ ϨⲘ̄ ⲠⲈϤⲞⲨⲰϢ ⲞⲨ ⲘⲞⲚⲞⲚ ϪⲈ Ⲛ̄ⲦⲀⲢⲈϤ

ⲞⲨⲰⲚϨ ⲈⲂⲞⲖ ⲀϤⲔⲰ Ⲛ̄ⲦⲮⲨⲬⲎ Ⲛ̄ⲦⲀⲢⲈϤ`

ⲞⲨⲰϢ ⲀⲖⲖⲀ ϪⲒⲘ ⲪⲞⲞⲨ ⲈⲠⲔⲞⲤⲘⲞⲤ ϢⲞ

ⲞⲠ' ⲀϤⲔⲰ Ⲛ̄ⲦⲮⲨⲬⲎ Ⲙ̄ⲠⲤⲞⲠ ⲈⲦⲈϤ'ⲞⲨ

10 ⲰϢ' ⲦⲞⲦⲈ ⲀϤⲈⲒ Ⲛ̄ϢⲞⲢⲠ' ⲈϤⲚⲀϤⲒⲦⲤ̄ ⲈⲠⲈⲒ

Ⲛ̄ⲦⲀⲨⲔⲀⲀⲤ Ⲛ̄ⲚⲈⲞⲨⲰ · ⲀⲤϢⲰⲠⲈ ϨⲀ ⲚⲖⲎ

ⲤⲦⲎⲤ ⲀⲨⲰ ⲀⲨϤⲒⲦⲤ̄ Ⲛ̄ⲀⲒⲬⲘⲀⲖⲰⲦⲞⲤ ⲀϤⲚⲞϨ

ⲘⲈⲤ ⲆⲈ ⲀⲨⲰ ⲚⲈⲦⲚⲀⲚⲞⲨⲞⲨ ϨⲘ̄ ⲠⲔⲞⲤⲘ.ⲞⲤ.

ⲀϤⲤⲞⲦⲞⲨ ⲀⲨⲰ ⲚⲈⲐⲞⲞⲨ ⲠⲞⲨⲞⲈⲒⲚ Ⲙ̄Ⲛ̄ ⲠⲔⲀ

15 ⲔⲈ ⲠⲰⲚϨ Ⲙ̄Ⲛ̄ ⲠⲘⲞⲨ Ⲛ̄ⲞⲨⲚⲀⲘ' Ⲙ̄Ⲛ̄ Ⲛ̄ϨⲂⲞⲨⲢ

Ⲛ̄ⲤⲚⲎⲨ ⲚⲈ Ⲛ̄ⲚⲞⲨⲈⲢⲎⲨ Ⲙ̄Ⲛ̄ ϬⲞⲘ Ⲛ̄ⲤⲈⲠⲰⲢϪ

ⲀⲚⲞⲨⲈⲢⲎⲨ ⲈⲦⲂⲈ ⲠⲀⲈⲒ ⲞⲨⲦⲈ ⲚⲈⲦⲚⲀⲚⲞⲨ

ⲞⲨ ⲚⲀⲚⲞⲨⲞⲨ ⲞⲨⲦⲈ ⲚⲈⲐⲞⲞⲨ ⲤⲈϨⲞⲞⲨ

ⲞⲨⲦⲈ ⲠⲰⲚϨ ⲞⲨⲰⲚϨ ⲠⲈ ⲞⲨⲦⲈ ⲠⲘⲞⲨ ⲞⲨ

[PAGE 55, PLATE 101]

It is not only at the time of his manifestation

that he made an offering of his life,

but since the beginning of the world that he gave his life

    in offering.

In the hour of his desire

He came to deliver this offering held captive.

It had been imprisoned by those who steal life for

    themselves.

He revealed the powers of the Gift,

and brought goodness to the heart of the wicked.

10   Light and darkness, life and death, right and left, are brothers

    and sisters. They are inseparable.

This is why goodness is not always good,

violence not always violent, life not always enlivening,

death not always deadly . . .

20 ΜΟΥ ΠΕ ΔΙΑ ΤΟΥΤΟ ΠΟΥΑ ΠΟΥΑ ΝΑΒΩΛ
ΕΒΟΛ · ΑΤΕϤΑΡΧΗ ΧΙΝ ϢΟΡΝ · ΝΕΤΧΟΣΕ
ΔΕ ΑΠΚΟΣΜΟΣ ΣⲚΝΑΤΒΩΛ ΕΒΟΛ ΝΕ
ΣⲚϢΑ ΕΝΕΣ ΝΕ ⲚΡΑΝ ΕΤΟΥ† ⲘΜΟΟΥ Ⲁ̄
ΚΟΣΜΙΚΟΣ ΟΥⲚΤΕΥ ⲘΜΑΥ ⲚΟΥΝΟϬ Ⲙ̄
25 ΠΛΑΝΗ ΣΕΠΩϢⳞ ΓΑΡ ⲘΠΟΥΣΗΤ· ΕΒΟΛ
ΣⲚ ΝΕΤΣΜΟΝΤ· ΕΣΟΥΝ ΕΝΕΤΣΜΟΝΤ·
ΑΝ ΑΥΩ ΠΕΤΣΩΤⲘ ΕΠΝΟΥΤΕ ΕϤΝΟ
ΕΙ ΑΝ ⲘΠΕΤΣΜΟΝΤ· ΑΛΛΑ ΑϤⲢΝΟΕΙ Ⲙ̄
ΠΕΤΣΜΟΝΤ ΑΝ ΤΕΕΙΣΕ ΟΝ ⲘΠΕΙΩΤ·
30 ΜⲚ ΠϢΗΡΕ ΜⲚ ΠΠ[Ⲛ].Ⲁ̄. ΕΤΟΥΑΑΒ ΜⲚ
ΠΩΝΣ ΜⲚ ΠΟΥΟΕΙ.Ⲛ. ΑΥΩ ΤΑΝΑΣΤΑ
ΣΙΣ ΜⲚ ΤΕΚΚΛΗΣΙ[Α ΜⲚ] ⲚΚΟΟΥΕ ΤΗΡΟΥ
ΕΥⲢΝΟΕΙ ΑΝ ⲚΝΕ[ΤΣΜΟ].Ⲛ.Τ· ΑΛΛΑ ΕΥⲢ
ΝΟΕΙ ⲚΝΕΤΣΜΟΝ[Τ ΑΝ ΠΛ]ΗΝ· ΑΥΣΕ
35 ΒΟ ΑΝΕΤΣΜΟΝΤ· Ρ.Ρ.[ΑΝ ΝΤΑΥΣΩ].ΤΜΟΥ.
ΣΕϢΟΟΠ· ΣⲘ ΠΚΟΣΜΟ[Σ ⲚΤΑΡΟΥⲢ]

All that is composite will decompose

and return to its Origin;

but those who are awake to the Reality

without beginning or end know the uncreated, the eternal.

11   The words we give to earthly realities engender illusion, they
turn the heart away from the Real to the unreal. The one
who hears the word *God* does not perceive the Real, but an
illusion or an image of the Real.

The same for the words *Father, Son, Holy Spirit, Life, Light,
Resurrection, Church,* and all the rest. These words do not
speak Reality;

we will understand this on the day

when we experience the Real.

All the words we hear in this world only deceive us.

If they were in the Temple Space [*Aeon*] they would keep
silent

and no longer refer to worldly things,

in the Temple Space [*Aeon*] they fall silent.

[PAGE 56, PLATE 102]

[ΑΠΑ].ΤΑ. [ΕΝΕΥ].Ψ.[Ο]ΟΠ ϨⲘ ΠΑΙⲰΝ ΝΕΥΝΑ
[Ⲣ]ΟΝΟΜΑ[ΖΕ].ΑΝ. ϨⲘ ΠⲔΟⲤΜΟⲤ ⲀⲖⲀⲀⲨ Ⲛ
ϨΟΟΥ ΟΥⲦ.Ε. .Ⲙ.ΠΟΥⲔⲀⲀΥ ϨⲚ ⲚϨⲂⲎΥΕ Ⲛ
ⲔΟⲤΜΙⲔΟΝ ΟΥⲚⲦΑΥ ⲘⲘΑΥ ⲚΝΟΥϨⲀⲎ ϨⲘ
5 ΠΑΙⲰΝ ΟΥⲢΑΝ ΟΥⲰⲦ‘ ΜΑΥⲦΕΥΟΥΑϤ‘
ϨⲘ ΠⲔΟⲤΜΟⲤ ΠⲢΑΝ ⲚⲦΑΠΕΙⲰⲦ‘ ⲦΑΑϤ‘
ⲘΠϢⲎⲢΕ ϤϪΟⲤΕ ΕΟΥΟΝ ΝΙΜ ΕⲦΕ ΠΑ
ΕΙ ΠΕ ΠⲢΑΝ ⲘΠΕΙⲰⲦ ΝΕⲢΕΠϢⲎⲢΕ ΓΑⲢ‘
ΝΑϢⲰΠΕ ΑΝ‘ ΕΙⲰⲦ ⲤΑⲂⲎⲖ ϪΕ ΑϤϮ ϨΙ
10 ⲰΟϤ‘ ⲘΠⲢΑΝ ⲘΠΕΙⲰⲦ‘ ΠΕΕΙⲢΑΝ ΝΕ
ⲦΕΥⲚⲦΑΥϤ ⲤΕⲢΝΟΕΙ ΜΕΝ ⲘΜΟϤ ⲤΕϢΑ
ϪΕ ⲆΕ ΕⲢΟϤ ΑΝ ΝΕⲦΕ ⲘⲚⲦΑΥϤ ⲆΕ ⲤΕ
ⲢΝΟΕΙ ⲘΜΟϤ ΑΝ ΑⲖⲖΑ ΑⲦΜΕ ϪΠΕ ϨΕΝΡⲀ
ϨⲘ ΠⲔΟⲤΜΟⲤ ΕⲦⲂⲎⲦⲚΝΑΕΙ ΕΜⲚ ϬΟΜ‘
15 ΑⲤΕⲂΟ ΕⲢΟⲤ ΧⲰⲢΙⲤ ⲢⲢΑΝ ΟΥΕΙ ΟΥⲰⲦ‘
ⲦΕ ⲦΜΕ ⲤΟ ⲚϨΑϨ ΑΥⲰ ΕⲦⲂⲎⲦⲚ ΕⲦⲤΕ
ⲂΟ ΕΠΑΕΙ ΟΥΑΑϤ‘ ϨⲚ ΟΥΑΓΑΠⲎ ϨΙⲦⲚ
ϨΑϨ ΑΝΑⲢΧⲰΝ ΟΥⲰϢ ΑⲢΑΠΑⲦΑ Ⲙ
ΠⲢⲰΜΕ ΕΠΕΙⲆⲎ ΑΥΝΑΥ ΕⲢΟϤ‘ ΕΥⲚⲦΑϤ‘

[PAGE 56, PLATE 102]

12   There is a name which is not heard in the world: It is the name that the Father gave to the Son; it is above everything, it expresses the Father. The Son would not be near the Father if the Father had not given him his name. Those who bear this name within them do not speak of it.

Those who do not bear it within them know nothing of it.

The Truth makes use of words in the world

because without these words, it would remain totally unknowable.

The Truth is one and many,

so as to teach us the innumerable One of Love.

20 ⲘⲘⲀⲨ Ⲛ̄ⲚⲞⲨⲤⲨⲄⲄⲈⲚⲈⲒⲀ ϢⲀ ⲚⲈⲦⲚⲀ
    ⲚⲞⲨⲞⲨ ⲚⲀⲘⲈ ⲀⲨϤⲒ ⲠⲢⲀⲚ Ⲛ̄ⲚⲈⲦⲚⲀ
    ⲚⲞⲨⲞⲨ ⲀⲨⲦⲀⲀϤ ⲀⲚⲈⲦⲚⲀⲚⲞⲨⲞⲨ ⲀⲚ·
    ϪⲈⲔⲀⲀⲤ ⲌⲒⲦⲚ̄ Ⲣ̄ⲢⲀⲚ ⲈⲨⲚⲀⲢ̄ⲀⲠⲀⲦⲀ Ⲙ̄
    ⲘⲞⲨ · ⲀⲨⲰ Ⲛ̄ⲤⲈⲘⲞⲢⲞⲨ ⲈⲌⲞⲨⲚ· ⲀⲚⲈⲦⲚⲀ
25 ⲚⲞⲨⲞⲨ ⲀⲚ ⲀⲨⲰ Ⲙ̄ⲘⲚ̄Ⲛ̄ⲤⲰⲤ ⲈϢϪⲈ ⲈⲨ
    ⲈⲒⲢⲈ ⲚⲀⲨ Ⲛ̄ⲞⲨⲌⲘⲞⲦ· Ⲛ̄ⲤⲈⲦⲢⲞⲨⲤⲈⲌⲰⲞⲨ
    ⲈⲂⲞⲖ Ⲛ̄ⲚⲈⲦⲚⲀⲚⲞⲨⲞⲨ ⲀⲚ ⲀⲨⲰ Ⲛ̄ⲤⲈ
    ⲔⲀⲀⲨ ⲌⲚ̄ ⲚⲈⲦⲚⲀⲚⲞⲨⲞⲨ ⲚⲀⲈⲒ ⲚⲈⲨⲤⲞ
    ⲞⲨⲚ Ⲙ̄ⲘⲞⲞⲨ ⲚⲈⲨⲞⲨⲰϢ ⲄⲀⲢ ⲈⲦⲢⲞⲨ
30 ϤⲒ ⲠⲈⲖⲈⲨⲐⲈⲢ[Ⲟ]Ⲥ Ⲛ̄ⲤⲈⲔⲀⲀϤ· ⲚⲀⲨ Ⲛ̄
    ⲌⲘϨⲀ̄Ⲗ̄ ϢⲀ ⲈⲚ[Ⲉ]Ⲍ ⲞⲨⲚ ⲌⲚ̄ⲆⲨⲚⲀⲘⲒⲤ
    ϢⲞⲞⲠ· ⲈⲨⲦⲒ[ⲚⲎ ⲈⲠ].Ⲉ̣Ⲓ̣.ⲢⲰⲘⲈ ⲈⲤⲈⲞⲨⲰϢ
    ⲀⲚ· ⲀⲦⲢⲈϤ·Ⲟ̣Ⲩ.[ϪⲀⲈⲒ] .Ⲭ̣.ⲈⲔⲀⲀⲤ ⲈⲨⲚⲀϢ
    ⲠⲈ Ⲉ.ⲬⲘ.[ⲠⲌⲘϨⲀ]Ⲗ ⲈⲢϢⲀⲠⲢⲰⲘⲈ ⲄⲀⲢ
35 .ⲞⲨⲞ.[ϢⲞⲨ ⲈⲨⲚⲀ] ϢⲰⲠⲈ Ⲛ̄ϬⲒ ⲌⲚ̄ⲐⲨⲤⲒⲀ
    [Ⲛ̄ⲌⲚⲐⲎⲢⲒⲞⲚ] ⲀⲨⲰ ⲚⲈⲨⲦⲀⲖⲈ ⲐⲎⲢⲒⲞⲚ·

13 High spiritual powers [*arkón*] wanted

to deceive humanity, because they saw goodness

engendered in Him.

They took the name for goodness

and applied it to what was not good;

words become deceitful,

and then are joined to that which is without being and without

goodness.

They alienate with simulations and appearances;

they make a free person into a slave.

14 These harmful powers do not want human beings to be saved;
they instill in them a taste for sacrifices; people then offer
animals to these powers; what was living becomes dead, and
their offering becomes a murder. But the *Anthropos*[39] who
offers himself to God can be killed: he is living.

---

39. [Here, the author prefers to import the word for *human being* from the original Greek.
In the context of this gospel, *anthropos* refers to a realized human being, whether man or
woman. It is not to be confused with *andros,* a man. Likewise, a Son of Man, though in
the masculine gender, might also refer to a woman. —*Trans.*]

[PAGE 57, PLATE 103]

ⲈⲌⲢⲀⲒ ⲚⲚⲆⲨⲚⲀⲘⲒ.Ⲥ. Ⲛ̣.Ⲑ̣.[Ⲉ] .Ⲛ̣.[ⲐⲎ].ⲢⲒ.ⲞⲚ .Ⲛ̣.[ⲀⲈⲒ]
ⲚⲈ ⲚⲈⲦⲞⲨⲦⲈⲖⲞ ⲈⲌⲢⲀⲒ ⲚⲀ[Ⲩ] ⲚⲈⲨⲦⲈⲖⲞ
ⲘⲈⲚ ⲘⲘⲞⲞⲨ ⲈⲌⲢⲀⲒ ⲈⲨⲞⲚ[Ⲍ] ⲚⲦⲀⲢⲞⲨⲦⲈ
ⲖⲞⲞⲨ ⲆⲈ ⲈⲌⲢⲀⲒ ⲀⲨⲘⲞⲨ ⲠⲢⲰⲘⲈ ⲀⲨⲦⲈⲖⲞϤ
5   ⲈⲌⲢⲀⲒ ⲘⲠⲚⲞⲨⲦⲈ ⲈϤⲘⲞⲞⲨⲦ' ⲀⲨⲰ ⲀϤⲰⲚⲌ
ⲌⲀ ⲦⲈⲌⲎ ⲈⲘ'ⲠⲀⲦⲈⲠⲈⲬ̅Ⲥ̅ ⲈⲒ ⲚⲈⲘⲚ̄ ⲞⲈⲒⲔ'
ⲌⲘ̄ ⲠⲔⲞⲤⲘⲞⲤ ⲚⲐⲈ ⲘⲠⲠⲀⲢⲀⲆⲒⲤⲞⲤ ⲠⲘ.Ⲁ.
ⲚⲈⲢⲈⲀⲆⲀⲘ ⲘⲘⲀⲨ ⲚⲈⲨⲚ̄ⲦⲀϤ ⲌⲀⲌ Ⲛ̄ⲮⲎⲚ
Ⲛ̄Ⲛ̄ⲦⲢⲞⲪⲎ Ⲛ̄Ⲛ̄ⲐⲎⲢⲒⲞⲚ ⲚⲈⲘⲚ̄ⲦⲀϤ ⲤⲞⲨⲞ
10 Ⲛ̄ⲦⲦⲢⲞⲪⲎ ⲘⲠⲢⲰⲘⲈ ⲚⲈⲢⲈⲠⲢⲰⲘⲈ ⲤⲞ
ⲈⲒⲰ Ⲛ̄ⲐⲈ Ⲛ̄Ⲛ̄ⲐⲎⲢⲒⲞⲚ' ⲀⲖⲖⲀ Ⲛ̄ⲦⲀⲢⲈⲠⲈⲬ̅Ⲥ̅
ⲈⲒ · ⲠⲦⲈⲖⲒⲞⲤ Ⲣ̄ⲢⲰⲘⲈ ⲀϤⲈⲒⲚⲈ Ⲛ̄ⲞⲨⲞⲈⲒⲔ'
ⲈⲂⲞⲖ ⲌⲚ̄ ⲦⲠⲈ ⲮⲒⲚⲀ ⲈⲢⲈⲠⲢⲰⲘⲈ ⲚⲀⲢ̄ⲦⲢⲈ
ⲪⲈⲤⲐⲀⲒ ⲌⲚ̄ ⲦⲦⲢⲞⲪⲎ ⲘⲠⲢⲰⲘⲈ ⲚⲈⲢⲈⲚ̄
15 ⲀⲢⲬⲰⲚ' ⲘⲈⲈⲨⲈ ϪⲈ ⲌⲚ̄ ⲦⲞⲨϬⲞⲘ' ⲘⲚ̄ ⲠⲞⲨ
ⲰⲮ ⲈⲨⲈⲒⲢⲈ Ⲛ̄ⲚⲈⲦⲞⲨⲈⲒⲢⲈ ⲘⲘⲞⲞⲨ ⲚⲈ
ⲢⲈⲠⲠⲚ̄Ⲁ̄ ⲆⲈ ⲈⲦⲞⲨⲀⲀⲂ ⲌⲚ̄ ⲞⲨⲠⲈⲐⲎⲠ'
ⲚⲈϤ'ⲈⲚⲈⲢⲄⲈⲒ ⲘⲠⲦⲎⲢϤ ⲈⲂⲞⲖ ⲌⲒⲦⲞⲞⲦⲞⲨ
Ⲛ̄ⲐⲈ ⲈⲦϤ'ⲞⲨⲰⲮ' ⲦⲀⲖⲎⲐⲈⲒⲀ ⲤⲈⲤⲒⲦⲈ ⲘⲘⲞⲤ

[PAGE 57, PLATE 103]

15   Before the coming of Christ there was no bread in the world.

In paradise, there were many trees to feed the animals;

humans fed themselves like animals.

There was no wheat

when Christ, the fulfilled Human, came;

He brought bread from heaven

so that humans would know a human food.

16   The high spiritual powers [*arkón*] thought that it was through

their power and their will that they did what they did; but

it was the Holy Spirit which, through them, worked its own

desire in secret.

The truth is sown everywhere, existing since the beginning;

some see it at the time it is sown,

but few still see it at the time of harvest.

20 ⲘⲘⲀ ⲚⲒⲘ ⲦⲈⲦⲰⲞⲞⲠ· ϪⲒⲚ ⲚϢⲞⲢⲠ ⲀⲨ
Ⲱ ⲞⲨⲚ ⲆⲀⲌ ⲚⲀⲨ ⲈⲢⲞⲤ ⲈⲨⲤⲒⲦⲈ ⲘⲘⲞⲤ ⲌⲚ
ⲔⲞⲨⲈⲒ ⲆⲈ ⲈⲦⲞⲨⲚⲀⲨ ⲈⲢⲞⲤ ⲈⲨⲰⲤⲌ ⲘⲘⲞⲤ
ⲠⲈϪⲈ ⲌⲞⲈⲒⲚⲈ ϪⲈ ⲀⲘⲀⲢⲒⲀ ⲱ̂ ⲈⲂⲞⲖ ⲌⲘ
ⲠⲠ̅Ⲛ̅Ⲁ̅ ⲈⲦⲞⲨⲀⲀⲂ· ⲤⲈⲢ̅ⲠⲖⲀⲚⲀⲤⲐⲈ ⲞⲨ ⲠⲈ
25 ⲦⲞⲨϪⲰ ⲘⲘⲞϤ· ⲤⲈⲤⲞⲞⲨⲚ ⲀⲚ ⲀⲨ Ⲛ̅ⲌⲞ
ⲞⲨ ⲈⲚⲈⲌ ⲠⲈⲚⲦⲀⲤⲌⲒⲘⲈ ⲱ̂ ⲈⲂⲞⲖ ⲌⲚ ⲤⲌⲒ
ⲘⲈ ⲘⲀⲢⲒⲀ ⲦⲈ ⲦⲠⲀⲢⲐⲈⲚⲞⲤ ⲈⲦⲈ ⲘⲠⲈ
ⲆⲨⲚⲀⲘⲒⲤ ϪⲀⲌⲘⲈⲤ ⲈⲤϢⲞⲞⲠ· Ⲛ̅ⲚⲞⲨ
ⲚⲞϬ Ⲛ̅ⲚⲀⲚⲞϢ Ⲛ̅Ⲛ̅ⲌⲈⲂⲢⲀⲒⲞⲤ ⲈⲦⲈ ⲚⲀ
30 ⲠⲞⲤⲦⲞⲖⲞⲤ ⲚⲈ ⲀⲨ.Ⲱ. [Ⲛ]ⲀⲠⲞⲤⲦⲞⲖⲒⲔⲞⲤ
ⲦⲈⲈⲒⲠⲀⲢⲐⲈ.ⲚⲞ.Ⲥ Ⲉ[ⲦⲈ] ⲘⲠⲈⲆⲨⲚⲀⲘⲒⲤ
ϪⲀⲌⲘⲈⲤ ⲞⲨ[ⲞⲂϢ ⲚⲦⲀⲚ]ⲚⲆⲨⲚⲀⲘⲒⲤ
ϪⲀⲌⲘⲞⲨ ⲀⲨⲰ .Ⲛ.[ⲈϤⲚⲀϪ].Ⲟ.ⲞⲤ ⲀⲚ Ⲛ̅ϬⲒ
ⲠϪⲞⲈⲒⲤ ϪⲈ ⲠⲀ.Ⲉ.[ⲒⲰⲦ ⲠⲈⲦⲌⲚ] ⲘⲠⲎⲨⲈ
35 ⲈⲒⲘⲎⲦⲒ ϪⲈ ⲚⲈⲨⲚ̅.Ⲧ.[ⲀϤ ⲘⲘⲀⲨ Ⲛ̅Ⲕ]ⲈⲈⲒⲰ.Ⲧ.
ⲀⲖⲖⲀ ⲌⲀⲠⲖⲰⲤ ⲀϤϪⲞ.Ⲟ.[Ⲥ ϪⲈ ⲠⲀⲈⲒⲰⲦ]
ⲠⲈϪⲈ ⲠϪⲞⲈⲒⲤ Ⲛ̅ⲘⲘⲀ.Ⲑ.[ⲎⲦⲎⲤ.......]

17   Some say that Mary was impregnated by the grace of the Holy
Spirit, but they do not know what they say.

How could the Feminine impregnate the feminine?

Mary is the virgin silence [*parthenos*]

which no evil power defiles or distracts;

she abides as the immaculate silence,

incomprehensible to the Hebrews, to the apostles, and to all
those who claim to be sent.

The Teacher would not have said: "My Father who is in
heaven,"

if he had not been engendered by another Paternity

than the one he had from his earthly father.

18   The Teacher said to his disciples:

". . . Enter into the house of the Father,

but bring nothing, and take nothing that is there."

[PAGE 58, PLATE 104]

[..].Ω.[...].Є.[.].N. ΜΕΝ Ι ЄϨΟΥΝ' ЄΠΗЄΙ
Μ̄ΠЄΙΩΤ [Μ]Π̄Р̄ϪΙ ΟΥΔЄ Ν̄ΤΟϤ' ϨΝ̄ ΠΗ
ЄΙ Μ̄ΠЄΙΩΤ Ν̄ΤЄΤΝ̄ϤΙ ЄΒΟΛ' ῙС̄ ΟΥΡᾹ
ΠЄ ЄϤϨΗΠ · ΠЄХР̄С̄ ΟΥΡΑΝ ΠЄ ЄϤΟΥΟΝϨ

5 ЄΒΟΛ ΔΙΑ ΤΟΥΤΟ ῙС̄ ΜΕΝ ϤϢΟΟΠ ΑΝ
ϨΝ̄ ΛΑΑΥ Ν̄ΝΑСΠЄ ΑΛΛΑ ΠЄϤΡΑΝ ΠЄ ῙΗ̄С̄
Ν̄ΘЄ ЄΤΟΥΜΟΥΤЄ ЄΡΟϤ Μ̄ΜΟС ΠЄХР̄С̄
ΔЄ ΠЄϤ'ΡΑΝ' ΠЄ Μ̄ΜΝ̄Τ̄СΥРΟС ΠЄ ΜЄС
СΙΑС Μ̄ΜΝ̄Τ̄ΟΥΑЄΙΑΝΙΝ ΔЄ ΠЄ ΠХ̄С̄ ΠᾹ

10 ΤΩС Ν̄ΚΟΟΥЄ ΤΗΡΟΥ ΟΥΝ̄ΤΑΥϤ' Μ̄ΜΑΥ
ΚΑΤΑ ΤΑСΠЄ Μ̄ΠΟΥΑ ΠΟΥΑ Ν̄ϨΗΤΟΥ'
ΠΝΑΖΑΡΗΝΟС ΠЄΤΟΥΟΝϨ ЄΒΟΛ ΠЄ
Μ̄ΠΠЄΘΗΠ · ΠЄХ̄С̄ ΟΥΝ̄ΤΑϤ' ΟΥΟΝ ΝΙΜ
ϨΡΑΪ̈ Ν̄ϨΗΤϤ' ЄΙΤЄ ΡΩΜЄ ЄΙΤЄ ΑΓ'ΓЄΛΟС

15 ЄΙΤЄ ΜΥСΤΗΡΙΟΝ ΑΥΩ ΠЄΙΩΤ' ΝЄΤϪΩ
Μ̄ΜΟС ϪЄ ΑΠϪΟЄΙС ΜΟΥ' Ν̄ϢΟΡΠ' ΑΥΩ
ΑϤΤΩΟΥΝ' СЄР̄ΠΛΑΝΑ ΑϤΤΩΟΥΝ ΓΑΡ'
Ν̄ϢΟΡΠ' ΑΥΩ ΑϤΜΟΥ ЄΤΜ̄ΟΥΑ ϪΠЄ
ΤΑΝΑСΤΑСΙС Ν̄ϢΟΡΠ' ϤΝΑΜΟΥ ΑΝ ϤΟΝϨ

[PAGE 58, PLATE 104]

19 Yeshua is a hidden name, Christ is a manifest name.

Yeshua cannot be translated into any language,

His name remains Yeshua;

Christ can be translated as *Messiah* in Hebrew and in Syriac,

Khristos in Greek;

each according to their tongue.

The Man of Nazareth is the visible of the invisible.

20 Christ contains all: man,

angel, mystery, Father.

21 Those who say that the Lord first died,

and then was resurrected, are wrong;

for he was first resurrected, and then died.

If someone has not first been resurrected, they can only die.

If they have already been resurrected, they are alive, as God is

Alive.

20 ⲚϬⲒ ⲠⲚⲞⲨⲦⲈ ⲚⲈⲢⲈⲠⲎ ⲚⲀⲘ'(ⲞⲨ) · ⲘⲀ̄ ⲀⲀ
ⲀⲨ ⲚⲀ2ⲰⲠ · ⲚⲚⲞⲨⲚⲞϬ ⲘⲠⲢⲀⲄⲘⲀ ⲈϤⲦⲀ
ⲈⲒⲎⲨ 2Ⲛ̄ ⲞⲨⲚⲞϬ Ⲛ̄2ⲰⲂ ⲀⲀⲀⲀ 2Ⲁ2 Ⲛ̄ⲤⲞⲠ'
ⲀⲞⲨⲀ 2Ⲛ̄ⲦⲂⲀ ⲈⲦⲈ ⲘⲚ̄ⲦⲞⲨ ⲎⲠⲈ ⲀϤⲚⲞⲬⲞⲨ
ⲀⲨ2ⲰⲂ 2Ⲁ ⲞⲨⲀⲤⲤⲀⲢⲒⲞⲚ ⲦⲀⲈⲒ ⲦⲈ ⲐⲈ Ⲛ̄
25 ⲦⲮⲨⲬⲎ ⲞⲨ2ⲰⲂ ⲈϤⲦⲀⲈⲒⲎⲨ ⲠⲈ ⲀⲤ Ⲱ
ⲠⲈ 2Ⲛ̄ ⲞⲨⲤⲰⲘⲀ ⲈϤ ⲎⲤ ⲞⲨⲚ̄ 2ⲞⲈⲒⲚⲈ
Ⲣ̄ 2ⲞⲦⲈ ⲬⲈ ⲘⲎⲠⲰⲤ Ⲛ̄ⲤⲈⲦⲰⲞⲨⲚ ⲈⲨⲔⲀ
Ⲕ Ⲁ2ⲎⲨ ⲈⲦⲂⲈ [ⲠⲈ]ⲈⲒ Ⲥ.Ⲉ.ⲞⲨⲰ ⲈⲦⲰⲞⲨⲚ
2Ⲛ̄ ⲦⲤⲀⲢⲜ ⲀⲨ.Ⲱ. [Ⲥ].ⲈⲤⲞⲞⲨ.Ⲛ ⲀⲚ ⲬⲈ ⲚⲈⲦⲢ̄
30 ⲪⲞⲢⲈⲒ Ⲛ̄ⲦⲤ[ⲀⲢⲜ ⲚⲦⲞⲞ]Ⲩ ⲠⲈ ⲈⲦⲔⲎⲔ Ⲁ2ⲎⲨ
ⲚⲀⲈⲒ ⲈⲦ.Ⲉ.[ⲨⲚⲀⲂⲰ] Ⲙ̄ⲘⲞⲞⲨ ⲈⲔⲀⲔⲞⲨ
Ⲉ2Ⲏ[Ⲩ ⲚⲦⲞⲞⲨ ⲠⲈ ⲈⲦⲔ]ⲀⲔ Ⲁ2ⲎⲨ ⲀⲚ ⲘⲚ̄ ⲤⲀⲢⲜ'
[2Ⲓ ⲤⲚⲞϤ ⲚⲀ].Ⲣ̄.ⲔⲀⲎⲢⲞⲚⲞⲘⲈⲒ Ⲛ̄ⲦⲘⲚ̄ⲦⲈ
[Ⲣ̄ⲢⲞ Ⲙ̄ⲠⲚⲞⲨ].Ⲧ.Ⲉ ⲚⲒⲘ' ⲦⲈ ⲦⲀⲈⲒ · ⲈⲦⲚⲀⲔⲀⲎ

22 No one hides a thing of great value in a vase which is too
   visible; treasures are hidden in inconspicuous pots.

   So it is with the soul, which is precious,

   and incarnated in perishable matter.

23 Some fear being revived while naked;

   this is why they want to be resurrected in their material body;

   they do not know that human beings are naked, with or

   without matter.

   They who make themselves simple, to the point of

   nakedness,

   are not naked.

   Neither flesh nor blood can inherit the Kingdom of God.[40]

   What is it that cannot inherit?

   It is the flesh and blood with which we identify;

   that which will inherit is the flesh and blood of Christ.

   He said it: "Those who do not eat my flesh

   and do not drink my blood have not life in them."[41]

---

40. Cf. 1 Cor 15:50.
41. Cf. John 6:53.

[PAGE 59, PLATE 105]

ⲢⲞⲚⲞⲘⲈⲒ ⲀⲚ ⲦⲀⲈⲒ ⲈⲦⲊⲒⲰⲚ ⲚⲒⲘ ⲆⲈ .Ⲧ.[Ⲉ
ⲦⲀⲈⲒ ⲌⲰⲞⲤ ⲈⲦⲚⲀⲔⲖⲎⲢⲞⲚⲞⲘⲈⲒ ⲦⲀ ⲒⲤ̄
ⲦⲈ ⲘⲚ̄ ⲠⲈⲨ‘ⲤⲚⲞⲨ · ⲆⲒⲀ ⲦⲞⲨⲦⲞ ⲠⲈⲬⲀⲨ ⲬⲈ
ⲠⲈⲦⲀⲞⲨⲰⲘ ⲀⲚ Ⲛ̄ⲦⲀⲤⲀⲢⲜ ⲀⲨⲰ Ⲛ̄ⲨⲤⲰ Ⲙ̄
5 ⲠⲀⲤⲚⲞⲨ · ⲘⲚ̄ⲦⲀⲨ ⲰⲚⲌ ⲌⲢⲀⲒ̈ Ⲛ̄ⲌⲎⲦϤ ⲀⲨ̈
ⲦⲈ ⲦⲈⲨ‘ⲤⲀⲢⲜ ⲠⲈ ⲠⲖⲞⲄⲞⲤ ⲀⲨⲰ ⲠⲈⲨ‘ⲤⲚⲞⲨ
ⲠⲈ ⲠⲠⲚ̄Ⲁ̄ ⲈⲦⲞⲨⲀⲀⲂ ⲠⲈⲚⲦⲀϪⲒ ⲚⲀⲈⲒ ⲞⲨ̈
ⲦⲈⲨ‘ⲦⲢⲞⲪⲎ ⲀⲨⲰ ⲞⲨⲚ̄ⲦⲀϤ‘ ⲤⲰ ⲌⲒ Ⲃ̄ⲤⲰ‘
ⲀⲚⲞⲔ ϮϬⲚ̄ ⲀⲢⲒⲔⲈ ⲀⲚⲔⲞⲞⲨⲈ ⲈⲦⲬⲰ ⲘⲘⲞⲤ
ⲬⲈ ⲤⲚⲀⲦⲰⲞⲨⲚ ⲀⲚ ⲈⲒⲦⲈ ⲚⲦⲞⲞⲨ Ⲙ̄ⲠⲈⲤ
ⲚⲀⲨ ⲤⲈϢⲞⲞⲠ Ⲍ̄Ⲛ ⲞⲨϢⲦⲀ   ⲔⲬⲰ Ⲙ̄ⲘⲞⲤ
ⲬⲈ ⲦⲤⲀⲢⲜ‘ ⲚⲀⲦⲞⲨⲚ ⲀⲚ ⲀⲖⲖⲀ ⲬⲞⲞⲤ ⲈⲢⲞ
ⲈⲒ ⲬⲈ ⲀⲨ̈ ⲠⲈⲦⲚⲀⲦⲰⲞⲨⲚ ϢⲒⲚⲀ ⲈⲚⲀⲦⲀ
ⲈⲒ̈ⲞⲔ ⲔⲬⲰ Ⲙ̄ⲘⲞⲤ ⲬⲈ ⲠⲠⲚ̄Ⲁ̄ Ⲍ̄Ⲛ ⲦⲤⲀⲢⲜ
15 ⲀⲨⲰ ⲠⲈⲈⲒⲔⲈⲞⲨⲞⲈⲒⲚ ⲠⲈ Ⲍ̄Ⲛ ⲦⲤⲀⲢⲜ ⲞⲨⲖⲞ
ⲄⲞⲤ ⲠⲈ ⲠⲈⲈⲒⲔⲈ ⲈϤⲌ̄Ⲛ ⲦⲤⲀⲢⲜ ⲬⲈ ⲠⲈⲦⲔⲚⲀ
ⲬⲞⲞⲤ ⲈⲔⲬⲈ ⲖⲀⲀⲨ ⲀⲚ Ⲙ̄ⲠⲂⲞⲖ Ⲛ̄ⲦⲤⲀⲢⲜ
ⲌⲀⲠⲤ̄ ⲠⲈ ⲈⲦⲞⲨⲚ Ⲍ̄Ⲛ ⲦⲈⲈⲒⲤⲀⲢⲜ‘ ⲈⲌⲰⲂ
ⲚⲒⲘ‘ ϢⲞⲞⲠ‘ Ⲛ̄ⲌⲎⲦⲤ̄ Ⲍ̄Ⲙ ⲠⲈⲈⲒⲔⲞⲤⲘⲞⲤ

[PAGE 59, PLATE 105]

What is his flesh?

His flesh is the Word [*Logos*];

his blood is the Breath [*pneuma*];

whoever welcomes the Word and the Breath

has truly received a food, a drink, and a garment.

I pity those who say there is no resurrection.

The flesh does not resurrect,

but what is it that can resurrect,

so that we revere it?

The Breath [*pneuma*] animates the flesh [*sarx*];

there is also this light in the flesh: the *Logos*.

What you say, you say in a body;

you can say nothing outside this body.

You must awaken while in this body, for everything exists in it:

Resurrect in this life.

20 ΝΕΤϯ ϨΙΩΟΥ ΝΝϨΒϹΩ ϹΕϹΟΤΠ' ΑΝΝ
ϨΒϹΩ ϨΝ ΤΜΝΤΕΡΟ ΝΜΠΗΥΕ ΝϨΒϹΩ
ϹΕϹΟΤΠ' ΑΝΕΝΤΑΥΤΑΑΥ ϨΙΩΟΥ ϨΙΤΝ
ΟΥΜΟΟΥ ΜΝ ΟΥΚΩϨΤ' ΕΥΤΟΥΒΟ ΜΠΜΑ
ΤΗΡϤ' ΝΕΤΟΥΟΝϨ ϨΙΤΝ ΝΕΤΟΥΟΝϨ Ε

25 ΒΟΛ ΝΕΘΗΠ' ϨΙΤΝ ΝΕΘΗΠ' ΟΥΝ ϨΟ
ΕΙΝΕ ΕΥϨΗΠ' ϨΙΤΝ ΝΕΤΟΥΟΝϨ ΕΒΟΛ
ΟΥΜ ΜΟΟΥ ϨΝ ΟΥΜΟΟΥ ΟΥΝ ΚΩϨΤ
ϨΝΝ ΟΥΧΡΙϹΜΑ ΑΙϹ ϤΙΤΟΥ ΝϪΙΟΥΕ
ΤΗΡΟΥ ΜΠΕϤ'ΟΥΩ[ΝϨ] ˌΓˌΑΡ ΕΒΟΛ' ΝΘΕ

30 ΕΝΕϤϢΟΟΠ' [ΝΑΜΕ Α]ΛΛΑ ΝΤΑϤΟΥΩΝϨ
ΕΒΟΛ ΝΘΕ ΕˌΤˌ[ΟΥΝΑϬ]ΜϬΟΜ ΝΝΑΥ
ΕΡΟϤ' ΝϨΗΤϹ Ν[ΑΙ ΤΗ]ˌΡˌΟΥ ΑϤΟΥ
ΩΝϨ ΕΒΟΛ ΝΑΥ Α[ϤΟΥΩΝϨ Ε]ˌΒˌΟΛ Ν
ΝΟϬ ϨΩϹ ΝΟϬ ΑϤΟΥ[ΩΝϨ ΕΒΟΛ Ν]

35 ΝΚΟΥΕΙ ϨΩϹ ΚΟΥΕΙ ΑϤ[ΟΥΩΝϨ ΕΒΟΛ]

24   In this world those who wear a garment

are more precious than their garment.

In the Kingdom of Heaven, the garments

are as precious as those who wear them,

for they have been immersed in a fire and in a water that
    purifies all.

25   That which can be visible is visible;

that which is secret remains secret;

yet certain secrets are revealed.

There is living water in baptismal water,

and a sacred fire in oils of anointment [*khrisma*].

26   Yeshua did not reveal himself as he is in reality, but according
    to the capacity of those who wanted to see Him.

He is the Unique for all,

yet to the great he appeared great, to the small he appeared
    small,

to the angels as an angel,

to human beings as a man.

The Logos is the secret of all.

Some who know themselves have known it.

[PAGE 60, PLATE 106]

[ΝΝ]ΑΓΓΕ[Λ].ΟC, ϨΩC ΑΓΓΕΛΟC ΑΥΩ
ΝῬΩΜΕ ϨΩC ῬΩΜΕ ΕΤΒΕ ΠΑΕΙ ΑΠΕϤ
ΛΟΓΟC ΑϤϨΟΠϤ· ΕΟΥΟΝ· ΝΙΜ ϨΟΕΙΝΕ
ΜΕΝ ΑΥΝΑΥ ΕΡΟΥ ΕΥΜΕΕΥΕ ΧΕ ΝΑΥΝΑΥ
5 ΕΡΟΟΥ ΜΜΙΝ ΜΜΟΟΥ · ΑΛΛΑ ΝΤΑΡΕϤ·ΟΥ
ΩΝϨ· ΕΒΟΛ ΝΝΕϤ·ΜΑΘΗΤΗC ϨΝ ΟΥΕΟ
ΟΥ ϨΙΧΜ ΠΤΟΟΥ ΝΕϤΟ ΑΝ ΝΚΟΥΕΙ ΑϤ·
ΨΩΠΕ ΝΝΟϬ ΑΛΛΑ ΝΤΑϤῬ ΜΜΑΘΗΤΗC
ΝΝΟϬ ΧΕΚΑΑC ΕΥΝΑΨ ϬΜϬΟΜ ΝΝΑΥ
10 ΕΡΟϤ· ΕϤΟ ΝΝΟϬ ΠΕΧΑϤ· ΜΦΟΟΥ ΕΤΜ
ΜΑΥ ϨΝ ΤΕΥΧΑΡΙCΤΕΙΑ ΧΕ ΠΕΝΤΑϨϨΩΤῬ
ΜΠΤΕΛΕΙΟC ΠΟΥΟΕΙΝ· ΕΠΠΝΑ ΕΤΟΥ
ΑΑΒ· ϨΟΤῬ ΝΑΓΓΕΛΟC· ΕΡΟΝ · ϨΩΩΝ ΑΝ
ϨΙΚΩΝ ΜΠῬΚΑΤΑΦΡΟΝΕΙ ΜΠϨΙΕΙΒ· ΑΧΝ
15 ΤϤ· ΓΑΡ · ΜΝ ΨϬΟΜ ΕΝΑΥ ΕΠΡΟ · ΜΝ ΛΑΑΥ
ΝΑΨ⳨ ΠΕϤΟΥΟΕΙ ΕϨΟΥΝ· ΕΠΡΡΟ ΕϤ·
ΚΗΚ ΑϨΗΥ · ΠῬΜΜΠΕ ΝΑΨΕ ΝΕϤΨΗΡΕ
ΝϨΟΥΟ ΑΠῬΜΝΚΑϨ ΕΨΧΕ ΝΨΗΡΕ ΝΑ
ΔΑΜ · ΝΑΨΩΟΥ ΚΑΙΤΟΙΓΕ ΨΑΥΜΟΥ ΠΟ

[PAGE 60, PLATE 106]

When he appeared to his disciples in glory on the mountain,

he was great, he was not small.

It was he who made his disciples great,

so that they would be able to see him in his grandeur.

That very day he said in his act of grace [*eukharistia*]:

"Thou who hast united fullness and light with Breath
[*pneuma*],

let our image and our angel be with us."

27 Do not despise the Sheep, for without him it is impossible to
see the door.

None can approach the King while naked.

28 The sons of heavenly Man outnumber

the sons of earthly man.

Though the sons of Adam are many, they are mortal;

the sons of the realized Man [*telleios*] never die,

for they are constantly being reborn.

20 ϹⲰ ⲘⲀⲖⲖⲞⲚ Ⲛ̄ϢⲎⲢⲈ Ⲙ̄ⲠⲦⲈⲖⲈⲒⲞϹ Ⲣ̄ⲢⲰ
ⲘⲈ ⲚⲀⲈⲒ ⲈⲘⲀⲨⲘⲞⲨ ⲀⲖⲖⲀ ϹⲈϪⲠⲞ Ⲙ̄ⲘⲞ
ⲞⲨ ⲞⲨⲞⲈⲒϢ ⲚⲒⲘ' ⲠⲈⲒⲰⲦ ⲦⲀⲘⲈⲒⲞ ϢⲎ
ⲢⲈ ⲀⲨⲰ ⲠϢⲎⲢⲈ' ⲘⲚ̄ ϬⲞⲘ Ⲙ̄ⲘⲞϤ' Ⲛ̄ϤⲦⲀ
ⲘⲒⲈ ϢⲎⲢⲈ ⲠⲈⲚⲦⲀⲨϪⲠⲞϤ ⲄⲀⲢ' ⲘⲚ̄ ϬⲞⲘ'
25 Ⲙ̄ⲘⲞϤ · Ⲛ̄ϤϪⲠⲞ ⲀⲖⲖⲀ ⲈⲠϢⲎⲢⲈ ϪⲠⲞ
ⲚⲀϤ' Ⲛ̄ϨⲚ̄ϹⲚⲎⲨ Ⲛ̄ϨⲚ̄ϢⲎⲢⲈ ⲀⲚ ⲚⲈⲦⲞⲨ
ϪⲠⲞ Ⲙ̄ⲘⲞⲞⲨ ⲦⲎⲢⲞⲨ Ϩ̄Ⲙ ⲠⲔⲞϹⲘⲞϹ
ⲈⲨϪⲠⲞ Ⲙ̄ⲘⲞ.Ⲟ.[Ⲩ] .Ⲉ.Ⲃ.ⲞⲖ. Ϩ̄Ⲛ ⲦϤⲨϹⲒϹ ⲀⲨ
Ⲱ Ⲛ̄ⲔⲞⲞⲨⲈ Ϩ.Ⲙ̄. [ⲠⲚ̄].Ⲁ̄. .Ⲛ.[ⲈⲦ].Ⲟ.ⲨϪⲠⲞ Ⲙ̄ⲘⲞⲞⲨ
30 ⲈⲂⲞⲖ' Ⲛ̄ϨⲎⲦ.Ϥ. [ϢⲀⲨⲦⲞⲈⲒ]Ϣ' ⲈⲂⲞⲖ' Ⲙ̄ⲘⲀⲨ
ⲈⲠⲢⲰⲘⲈ .Ϫ.[Ⲉ ⲈⲨϹⲞ].Ⲉ.ⲒϢ ⲈⲂⲞⲖ Ϩ̄Ⲙ ⲠⲢ̄
[Ⲣ]ⲎⲦ .ⲈϪ.[Ⲙ̄ ⲠⲦⲞ]ⲠⲞϹ Ⲙ̄ⲠϹⲀ ⲚⲦⲠⲈ
[ⲠⲈⲦϹⲞⲈⲒϢ Ⲙ̄]ⲘⲞϤ' ⲈⲂⲞⲖ Ϩ̄Ⲛ Ⲧ'ⲦⲀⲠⲢⲞ
[ⲀⲨⲰ ⲈⲚⲈⲢⲈ]ⲠⲖⲞⲄⲞϹ ⲈⲒ ⲈⲂⲞⲖ Ⲙ̄ⲘⲀⲨ

29 The father begot a son, the son did not beget a son.

Who has been begotten cannot beget.

The son begets brothers, not sons.

30 All those who are begotten in the world

are begotten by physical means;

the others are begotten by spiritual means.

Those who are begotten by Spirit [*pneuma*]

hope for the realization of Humanity;

they are nourished by the promise of a higher space [*topos*].

31 Those who are nourished by the word which comes to the
    mouth go toward their own realization.

The realized human is fertilized by a kiss,

and is born through a kiss.

This is why we kiss each other,

giving birth to each other

through the love [*kharis*, also grace] that is in us.

[PAGE 61, PLATE 107]

NEϤΝΑⲤΟΕΙϢ ΕΒΟ[Λ] ⳵Ñ TT.A.ПРО .AY.[Ω]
ΝΕϤΝΑϢⲰΠΕ ÑTΕΛΕΙΟⳄ ΝΤΕΛΕΙΟⳄ Γ.ΑΡ.
⳵ΙΤÑ ΟΥΠΕΙ ΕΥ⳽ ΑΥⲰ ΕΥⳘΠΟ ΔΙΑ ΤΟΥΤΟ
ΑΝΟΝ᾿ ⳵ⲰⲰΝ ΤÑ† ΠΙ ΕΡÑ ÑÑΝΕΡΗΥ
5   ΕΝⳘΙ ṀΠⳍ ΕΒΟΛ ⳵Ñ ΤⳘΑΡΙⳄ ΕΤ⳵Ñ Ν
ÑΝΕΡΗΥ ΝΕΟΥÑ ϢΟΜΤΕ ΜΟΟϢΕ ΜÑ
ΠⳘΟΕΙⳄ ΟΥΟΕΙϢ ΝΙΜ ΜΑΡΙΑ ΤΕϤΜΑΑΥ
ΑΥⲰ ΤΕⳄⳄⲰΝΕ ΑΥⲰ ΜΑΓΔΑΛΗΝΗ .Τ.Α
ΕΙ ΕΤΟΥΜΟΥΤΕ ΕΡΟⳄ ⳘΕ ΤΕϤΚΟΙΝⲰΝΟⳄ
10 ΜΑΡΙΑ ΓΑΡ ΤΕ ΤΕϤⳄⲰΝΕ ΑΥⲰ ΤΕϤ᾿ΜΑΑΥ
ΤΕ ΑΥⲰ ΤΕΥ⳵ⲰΤΡΕ ΤΕ ΠΕΙⲰΤ ΜÑ ΠϢΗ
ΡΕ Ñ⳵ΑΠΛΟΥΝ ΝΕ ₽ΡΑΝ ΠΠÑⲀ ΕΤΟΥΑΑΒ
ΟΥΡΑΝ᾿ ΠΕ ÑΔΙΠΛΟΥΝ ⳄΕϢΟΟΠ ΓΑΡ᾿ Ṁ
ΜΑ ΝΙΜ᾿ ⳄΕṀΠⳄΑ ΝΤΠΕ ⳄΕṀΠⳄΑ ΜΠΙ
15 ΤÑ ⳄΕ⳵Ñ ΠΕΘΗΠ᾿ ⳄΕ⳵Ñ ΝΕΤΟΥΟΝ⳵
ΕΒΟΛ ΠΠÑⲀ ΕΤΟΥΑΑΒ · ϤⳄṀ ΠΟΥⲰΝ⳵
ΕΒΟΛ · ϤⳄṀ ΠⳄΑ ΜΠΙΤÑ ϤⳄṀ ΠΕΘΗΠ᾿
ϤⳄṀ ΠⳄΑ ΝΤΠΕ ⳄΕϢṀϢΕ ÑΝΕΤΟΥ
ΑΑΒ · ⳵ΙΤÑ Ñ⳽ΥΝΑΜΙⳄ ṀΠΟΝΗΡΟΝ ·

[PAGE 61, PLATE 107]

32   There were three who always walked with the Lord:

Mary, his mother; the sister of his mother; and Miriam of
    Magdala,

known as his companion [*koinonos*];

for him, Miriam is a sister, a mother, and a wife [*koinonos*].

33   Father and son are simple [*aplous*] names;

The Breath is a double [*diplous*] name, for it is everywhere:

above, below, in the visible, in the invisible.

Spirit [*pneuma*] becomes manifest when descending,

and unmanifest when ascending.

34   The saints make use of harmful powers.

These powers are blinded by the Breath

to believe that they are using it,

whereas they are working for the saints.

One day a disciple asked the Teacher a question

about the state of the world.

20 CEO ΓΑΡ ΝΒΛΛΕ ϨΙΤΜ ΠΝᾱ ΕΤΟΥΑΑΒ
ΧΕΚΑΑC ΕΥΝΑΜΕΕΥΕ ΧΕ ΕΥⲢϨΥΠΗΡΕ
ΤΕΙ ΝΝΟΥⲢⲰΜΕ ϨΟΠΟΤΕ ΕΥΕΙΡΕ ΝΝΕ
ΤΟΥΑΑΒ · ΕΤΒΕ ΠΑΕΙ ΑΥΜΜΑΘΗΤΗC Ⲣ̄
ΑΙΤΕΙ ΜΠΧΟΕΙC ΝΝΟΥϨΟΟΥ ΕΤΒΕ ΟΥ
25 ϨⲰΒ ΝΤΕ ΠΚΟCΜΟC ΠΕΧΑϤ ΝΑϤ ΧΕ
ΕΡΙΑΙΤΕΙ ΝΤΕΚΜΑΑΥ ΑΥⲰ CΝΑ† ΝΑΚ
ΕΒΟΛ ϨΝ ΑΛΛΟΤΡΙΟΝ ΠΕΧΕ ΝΑΠΟCΤΟ
ΛΟC ΝΝΜΑΘΗΤΗC ΧΕ ΤΜΠΡΟCΦΟ
ΡΑ ΤΗΡⲤ̄ ΜΑΡΕCΧΠ[Ο Ν].Α.C ΝΟΥϨΜΟΥ·
30 ΝΕΥΜΟΥΤΕ [ΕΤCΟΦΙ].Α. ΧΕ ϨΜΟΥ ΑΧΝΤⲤ̄
ΜΑΡΕΠΡΟCΦ[ΟΡΑ ϢⲰΠ]Ε ΕϤϢΗΠ· ΤCΟ
ΦΙΑ ΔΕ ΟΥCΤΕΙΡ[Α ΤΕ ΑΧⲘ Π]ϢΗΡΕ ΔΙΑ ΤΟΥ
ΤΟ ΕΥΜΟΥΤΕ ΕΡΟ[C ΧΕ ΟΥ].C.ΕΠΕΙ Ν
ϨΜΟΥ ΠΜΑ ΕΤΟΥΝΑ.Ϣ.[CΟΕΙϢ ΝϨΗΤϤ]
35 ΝΤΟΥϨΕ ΠΠΝᾱ ΕΤΟΥΑΑ.Β. [ΠΕ ΔΙΑ ΤΟ]

He answered him: "Ask your mother; she will speak to you of
what is other [*allotrion*]."

35   The apostles [*apostolos*] said to the disciples [*mathetes*]:
"May our offerings [*prosphora*] contain salt."
They called Wisdom [*Sophia*] "salt."
Without it, no offering is acceptable.

36   But Wisdom is barren without the Son.
Hence salt is only a trace.
What nourishes them is the Breath [*pneuma*]
and its offspring are many.

37   What belongs to the father belongs to the son, but while he is
still young, he is not entrusted with all that is his.
When he is mature, his father gives it to him.

[PAGE 62, PLATE 108]

[ΥΤ].Ο. ΝΑΨ.Ε. ΝΕ.ϹΨΗ.ΡΕ ΠΕΤΕΥΝΤΑϤϤ`
.Ν.ϬΙ ΠΕΙΩΤ ΝΑ ΠΨΗΡΕ ΝΕ ΑΥΩ ΝΤΟϤ ϨΩ
ΩϤ · ΠΨΗΡΕ ΕΝ ϨΟϹΟΝ ϤΟ ΝΚΟΥΕΙ · ΜΑΥ
ΠΙϹΤΕΥΕ ΝΑϤ ΑΝΕΤΕ ΝΟΥϤ · ϨΟΤΑΝ ΕϤ`
5 ΨΑΨΩΠΕ ῬΡΩΜΕ ΨΑΡΕΠΕϤΕΙΩΤ Ϯ ΝΑϤ`
ΝΕΤΕΥΝΤΑΒϹΕ ΤΗΡΟΥ ΝΕΤϹΟΡΜ ΝΕΤΕ Π`
ΠΝΑ ΧΠΟ ΜΜΟΟΥ ΨΑΥϹΩΡΜ` ΟΝ` ΕΒΟΛ
ϨΙΤΟΟΤϤ` ΔΙΑ ΤΟΥΤΟ ΕΒΟΛ ϨΙΤΜ ΠΙΠΝΑ
ΟΥΩΤ` ϤΧΕΡΟ ΝϬΙ ΠΚΩϨΤ ΑΥΩ ϤΩΨΜ
10 ΚΕΟΥΑ ΠΕ ΕΧΑΜΩΘ ΑΥΩ ΚΕΟΥΑ ΠΕ`
ΕΧΜΩΘ ΕΧΑΜΩΘ ΤΕ ΤϹΟΦΙΑ ϨΑΠΛΩϹ
ΕΧΜΩΘ ΔΕ ΤΕ ΤϹΟΦΙΑ ΜΠΜΟΥ ΕΤΕ ΤΑ
ΕΙ ΤΕ ΤϹΟΦΙΑ ΜΠΜΟΥ ΕΤΕ ΤΑΕΙ ΤΕ ΕΤϹΟ
ΟΥΝ ΜΠΜΟΥ ΤΑΕΙ ΕΤΟΥΜΟΥΤΕ ΕΡΟϹ ΧΕ
15 ΤΚΟΥΕΙ ΝϹΟΦΙΑ ΟΥΝ ϨΝΘΗΡΙΟΝ ΨΟΟΠ`
ΕΥϨΥΠΟΤΑϹϹΕ ΜΠΡΩΜΕ ΝΘΕ ΜΠΜΑϹΕ
ΜΝ ΠΕΙΩ ΜΝ ϨΝΚΟΟΥΕ ΝΤΕΕΙΜΙΝΕ ΟΥ
Ν ϨΝΚΟΟΥΕ ΨΟΟΠ · ΕΥϨΥΠΟΤΑϹϹΕ ΑΝ`
ΕΥΟΥΑΤ` ϨΝ ΝΕΡΗΜΙΑ ΠΡΩΜΕ ϹΚΑΕΙ Ν

[PAGE 62, PLATE 108]

38 Those who are born of the spirit know not where they go; the same Breath lights and extinguishes the fire.

39 *Akhamoth* is one reality, and *Ekhmoth* is another. *Akhamoth* is ordinary wisdom,

Ekhmoth is the wisdom of death;

to know death is a small wisdom.

40 There are animals that obey people: the calf, the donkey, and those of this sort.

There are others who do not obey, and live apart in the wilderness.

People work with tame animals to plow their fields, and thus are able to feed themselves

and the animals, whether tame or wild.

20 ⲦⲤⲰϢⲈ ϨⲒⲦⲚ̄ Ⲛ̄ⲐⲎⲢⲒⲞⲚ ⲈⲦϨⲨⲠⲞⲦⲀⲤⲤⲈ
ⲀⲨⲰ ⲈⲂⲞⲖ ϨⲘ̄ ⲠⲀⲈⲒ ϤⲤⲞⲈⲒϢ 'Ⲛ̄ⲦⲞϤ' ⲘⲚ̄ Ⲛ̄
ⲐⲎⲢⲒⲞⲚ ⲈⲒⲦⲈ ⲚⲈⲦ'ϨⲨⲠⲞⲦⲀⲤⲤⲈ ⲈⲒⲦⲈ ⲚⲈⲦ'
ϨⲨⲠⲞⲦⲀⲤⲤⲈ ⲀⲚ ⲦⲀⲈⲒ ⲦⲈ ⲐⲈ Ⲙ̄ⲠⲦⲈⲖⲈⲒⲞⲤ
Ⲣ̄ⲢⲰⲘⲈ ϨⲒⲦⲚ̄ ϨⲚ̄ⲆⲨⲚⲀⲘⲒⲤ ⲈⲦϨⲨⲠⲞⲦⲀⲤ

25 ̣Ⲥ̣Ⲉ ⲈϤⲤⲔⲀⲈⲒ ⲞⲨⲞⲚ ⲚⲒⲘ' ⲈϤⲤⲞⲂⲦⲈ ⲈⲦⲢⲞⲨ
ϢⲰⲠⲈ ⲈⲦⲂⲈ ⲠⲀⲈⲒ ⲄⲀⲢ' ⲈⲠⲘⲀ ⲦⲎⲢϤ ⲀϨⲈ
ⲢⲀⲦϤ' ⲈⲒⲦⲈ ⲚⲈⲦⲚⲀⲚⲞⲨⲞⲨ ⲈⲒⲦⲈ ⲚⲈⲐⲞⲞⲨ
ⲀⲨⲰ ⲚⲞⲨⲚⲀⲘ' ⲘⲚ̄ Ⲛ̄ϬⲂⲞⲨⲢ ⲠⲈⲠⲚ̄Ⲁ̄ ⲈⲦⲞⲨ
ⲀⲀⲂ ϤⲘⲞⲞⲚⲈ [ⲞⲨⲞ]Ⲛ ⲚⲒⲘ' ⲀⲨⲰ ϤⲢ̄ⲀⲢⲬⲈⲒ

30 Ⲛ̄Ⲛ̄ⲆⲨⲚⲀⲘⲒⲤ Ⲧ[ⲎⲢⲞⲨ ⲚⲈ]̣Ⲧ̣ϨⲨⲠⲞⲦⲀⲤⲤⲈ
ⲀⲨⲰ ⲚⲈⲦϨⲨⲠ[ⲞⲦⲀⲤⲤⲈ Ⲁ]̣Ⲛ̣ ⲘⲚ̄ ⲚⲈⲦⲞⲨⲀⲦ'
ⲔⲀⲒ ⲄⲀⲢ ϤϬⲰ[Ⲗ Ⲙ̄ⲘⲞⲞⲨ Ϥ]ⲰⲦⲠ' Ⲙ̄ⲘⲞⲞⲨ Ⲉ
̣Ϩ̣ⲞⲨⲚ ϪⲈ [ⲈⲨⲚⲀϪⲒ ⲈϤ]̣Ϣ̣ⲀⲚⲞⲨⲰϢ ⲚⲞⲨϢ
[Ϭ]̣ⲞⲘ̣ [ⲀⲆⲀⲘ ⲈⲚⲈⲚⲦ]̣Ⲁ̣ⲨⲠⲖⲀⲤⲤⲈ Ⲙ̄ⲘⲞϤ ⲚⲈ

35 [ⲔⲚⲀ....ⲚⲈ]ⲔⲚⲀϨⲈ ⲀⲚⲈϤϢⲎⲢⲈ ⲈⲨⲞ

So it is with realized Human Beings, who work with energies
   that obey them.

They prepare all things to come into being.

Thus everything awakens, and is redeemed:

good and evil, right and left.

The Breath leads all things to their repose,

it aligns the energies: the obedient, the wild, and the solitary
   ones.

It gathers them together, so that

they are no longer dispersed.

41   The created one is beautiful, and his sons are noble.

[PAGE 63, PLATE 109]

ⲙⲡⲗⲁⲥⲙⲁ ⲛ̄ⲉⲩⲅⲉⲛⲏⲥ ⲉⲯⲭⲉ ⲙ̄ⲡⲟⲩ.ⲣ.
ⲡⲗⲁⲥⲥⲉ ⲙ̄ⲙⲟϥ · ⲁⲗⲗⲁ ⲁⲩϫⲡⲟϥ ⲛⲉⲕ'ⲛⲁ
ϩⲉ ⲁⲡⲉϥ'ⲥⲡⲉⲣⲙⲁ ⲉϥⲟ ⲛ̄ⲉⲩⲅⲉⲛⲏⲥ ⲧⲉ
ⲛⲟⲩ ⲇⲉ ⲁⲩⲡⲗⲁⲥⲥⲉ ⲙ̄ⲙⲟϥ' ⲁϥϫⲡⲟ ⲁⲩ
5 ⲛ̄ⲉⲩⲅⲉⲛⲉⲓⲁ ⲡⲉ ⲡⲁⲉⲓ · ϣⲟⲣⲡ' ⲁⲧⲙⲛ̄ⲧⲛⲟ
ⲉⲓⲕ ϣⲱⲡⲉ ⲙ̄ⲙⲛ̄ⲛ̄ⲥⲱⲥ ϥⲱⲧⲃⲉ ⲁⲩⲱ ⲁⲩ
ϫⲡⲟϥ' ⲉⲃⲟⲗ · ϩⲛ̄ ⲧⲙⲛ̄ⲧⲛⲟⲉⲓⲕ' ⲛⲉⲡϣⲏ
ⲣⲉ ⲅⲁⲣ' ⲙ̄ⲫⲟϥ' ⲡⲉ ⲇⲓⲁ ⲧⲟⲩⲧⲟ ⲁϥϣⲱⲡⲉ
ⲛ̄ϩⲁⲧⲃ̄ⲣⲱⲙⲉ ⲛ̄ⲑⲉ ⲙ̄ⲡⲉϥⲕⲉⲉⲓⲱⲧ' ⲁⲩ
10 ⲱ ⲁϥⲙⲟⲩⲟⲩⲧ' ⲙ̄ⲡⲉϥ'ⲥⲟⲛ ⲕⲟⲓⲛⲱⲛⲓⲁ ⲇⲉ
ⲛⲓⲙ' ⲛ̄ⲧⲁϣϣⲱⲡⲉ ⲉⲃⲟⲗ ϩⲛ̄ ⲛⲉⲧ̄ⲛⲉ ⲁⲛ' ⲛ̄
ⲛⲟⲩⲉⲣⲏⲩ ⲟⲩⲙⲛ̄ⲧⲛⲟⲉⲓⲕ' ⲧⲉ · ⲡⲛⲟⲩⲧⲉ
ⲟⲩϫⲅⲓⲧ ⲡⲉ ⲛ̄ⲑⲉ ⲛ̄ⲛ̄ϫⲱϭⲉ ⲉⲧⲛⲁⲛⲟⲩⲟⲩ
ϣⲁⲩⲙⲟⲩⲧⲉ ⲉⲣⲟⲟⲩ ϫⲉ ⲛⲁⲗⲏⲑⲓⲛⲟⲛ ϣⲁⲩ
15 ⲙⲟⲩ ⲙⲛ̄ ⲛⲉⲛ'ⲧⲁⲩϫⲱϭⲉ ϩⲣⲁⲓ ⲛ̄ϩⲏⲧⲟⲩ ⲧⲁ
ⲉⲓ ⲧⲉ ⲑⲉ ⲛ̄ⲛⲉⲛ'ⲧⲁⲡⲛⲟⲩⲧⲉ ϫⲟϭⲟⲩ · ⲉ
ⲡⲉⲓⲇⲏ ϩⲛ̄ⲛⲁⲧ'ⲙⲟⲩ ⲛⲉ ⲛⲉϥϫⲱϭⲉ ϣⲁⲩ
ⲣ̄ ⲁⲧⲙⲟⲩ ⲉⲃⲟⲗ' ϩⲓⲧⲟⲟⲧϥ' ⲛ̄ⲛⲉϥⲡⲁϩⲣⲉ
ⲡⲛⲟⲩⲧⲉ ⲇⲉ ⲣ̄ⲃⲁⲡⲧⲓⲍⲉ ⲛ̄ⲛⲉⲧϥⲣ̄ⲃⲁⲡⲧⲓ

[PAGE 63, PLATE 109]

If he had been begotten, and not merely created,

you would find his seed even nobler;

but if he had been both created and begotten—what nobility!

42　First came adultery, then murder;

murder is the son of adultery, son of the serpent;

he is a murderer like his father, and killed his brother.

The mating [*koinonia*] of those who are dissimilar is adultery.

43　God is a dyer;

the good dyes, known as genuine,

become one with the materials that they permeate.

This is how God acts.

He gives his own colors to his dyes,

the colors of immortality.

Thus he baptizes us in water.

20 ⲍⲉ ⲘⲘⲞⲞⲨ ⲌⲚ ⲞⲨⲘⲞⲞⲨ ⲘⲚ ϬⲞⲘ'
ⲚⲦⲈⲖⲀⲀⲨ ⲚⲀⲨ ⲀⲖⲀⲀⲨ ⲌⲚ ⲚⲈⲦ'ⲤⲘⲞⲚⲦ'
ⲈⲒⲘⲎⲦⲒ ⲚⲦⲈⲠⲈⲦⲘⲘⲀⲨ ⲰⲰⲠⲈ ⲚⲐⲈ
ⲚⲚⲈⲦⲘⲘⲀⲨ ⲚⲐⲈ ⲘⲠⲢⲰⲘⲈ ⲀⲚ ⲈϤ
ⲌⲘ ⲠⲔⲞⲤⲘⲞⲤ ϤⲚⲀⲨ ⲈⲠⲢⲎ ⲈϤⲞ ⲢⲢⲎ
25 ⲀⲚ ⲀⲨⲰ ϤⲚⲀⲨ ⲈⲦⲠⲈ ⲘⲚ ⲠⲔⲀⲌ ⲘⲚ Ⲛ
ⲔⲈⲌⲂⲎⲨⲈ ⲦⲎⲢⲞⲨ ⲈⲚⲦⲞϤ' ⲀⲚ ⲠⲈ ⲚⲈⲦⲘ
ⲘⲀⲨ ⲦⲀⲈⲒ ⲦⲈ ⲐⲈ ⲌⲢⲀⲒ ⲌⲚ ⲦⲘⲈ ⲀⲖⲖⲀ ⲀⲔ
ⲚⲀⲨ ⲈⲖⲀⲀⲨ ⲚⲦⲈ ⲠⲘⲀ ⲈⲦⲘⲘⲀⲨ ⲀⲔⲰⲰ
ⲠⲈ ⲚⲚⲈⲦⲘⲘⲀⲨ · ⲀⲔⲚⲀ[Ⲩ] ⲀⲠⲠⲚⲀ ⲀⲔ'
30 ⲰⲰⲠⲈ ⲘⲠⲚⲀ .ⲀⲔ.Ⲛ[ⲀⲨ Ⲁ]ⲠⲬⲤ ⲀⲔⲰⲰⲠⲈ
ⲚⲬⲤ ⲀⲔⲚⲀⲨ Ⲁ[ⲠⲈⲒⲰⲦ Ⲕ]ⲚⲀⲰⲰⲠⲈ ⲚⲈⲒ
ⲰⲦ' ⲆⲒⲀ ⲦⲞⲨⲦⲞ [ⲘⲠⲘⲀ ⲠⲀⲈⲒ] ⲘⲈⲚ ⲔⲚⲀⲨ
ⲀⲌⲰⲂ ⲚⲒⲘ · ⲀⲨⲰ [ⲔⲚⲀⲨ ⲈⲢⲞⲔ]' ⲀⲚ ⲞⲨⲀⲀⲔ'
ⲔⲚⲀⲨ ⲆⲈ ⲈⲢⲞⲔ' Ⲙ[ⲠⲘⲀ ⲈⲦⲘ].Ⲙ.ⲀⲨ ⲠⲈⲦ
35 ⲔⲚⲀⲨ ⲄⲀⲢ' ⲈⲢⲞϤ' ⲈⲔⲚⲀ.Ⲱ.[ⲰⲰⲠⲈ ⲘⲘ].ⲞϤ.
ⲦⲠⲒⲤⲦⲒⲤ ϪⲒ ⲦⲀⲄⲀⲠⲎ' Ⲥ† .Ⲙ.[Ⲛ ⲖⲀⲀⲨ ⲚⲀⲰ]

44　It is impossible for anyone to see the everlasting reality and not
　　　become like it.

The Truth is not realized like truth in the world:

Those who see the sun do not become the sun;

those who see the sky, the earth, or anything that exists, do
　　　not become what they see.

But when you see something in this other space,

you become it.

If you know the Breath, you are the Breath.

If you know the Christ, you become the Christ.

If you see the Father, you are the Father.

[PAGE 64, PLATE 110]

[ⳈⲒ] ⳹Ⲁ⳹ ⳈⲚ ⲦⲠⳘⲒⳘⲤⲦⲒⲤ ⳘⲘⳘⲚ ⲖⲀⲀⲨ ⲚⲀϢ ✝ ⲀⳈⲚ
ⲀⲄⲀⲠⲎ ⲈⲦⲂⲈ ⲠⲀⲈⲒ ⳘⲈⲔⲀⲀⲤ ⲘⲈⲚ ⲈⲚⲀⳘⲒ
ⲦⲚⲠⲠⲒⲤⲦⲈⲨⲈ Ϣ︤ⲒⲚⲀ ⲆⲈ ⲚⲀⲘⲈ ⲚⲦⲚⳘ✝ ⲈⲠⲈⲒ
ⲈⲢϢⲀⲞⲨⲀ ✝ ⳈⲚ ⲞⲨⲀⲄⲀⲠⲎ ⲀⲚ ⲘⲚⲦⲈϤ Ω

5 ⲪⲈⲖⲈⲒⲀ ⳈⲘ̄ ⲠⲈⲚⲦⲀϤⲦⲀⲀϤ' ⲠⲈⲚⲦⲀⳈⲒ
ⲠⳈⲞⲈⲒⲤ ⲀⲚ ⲞⲚ Ⲛ̄ⳈⲈⲂⲢⲀⲒⲞⲤ ⲈⲦⲒ Ⲛ̄ⲀⲠⲞ
ⲤⲦⲞⲖⲞⲤ ⲈⲦⳈⲒⲦⲚ̄ⲚⲈⳈ ⲦⲈⲈⲒⳈⲈ ⲚⲈⲨⲘⲞⲨ
ⲦⲈ ⳘⲈ Ⲓ︤Ⲥ︥ ⲠⲚⲀⳈΩⲢⲀⲒⲞⲤ ⲘⲈⲤⲤⲒⲀⲤ ⲈⲦⲈ
ⲠⲀⲈⲒ ⲠⲈ Ⲓ︤Ⲏ︤Ⲥ︥ ⲠⲚⲀⳈΩⲢⲀⲒⲞⲤ ⲠⲈ︤Ⳉ︥ ⲠⳈⲀⲈ

10 Ⲣ̄ⲢⲀⲚ ⲠⲈ ⲠⲈⳈ︤Ⲥ︥ ⲠϢⲞⲢⲠ' ⲠⲈ Ⲓ︤Ⲥ︥ ⲠⲈⲦⳈⲚ̄
ⲦⲘⲎⲦⲈ ⲠⲈ ⲠⲚⲀⳈⲀⲢⲎⲚⲞⲤ ⲘⲈⲤⲤⲒⲀⲤ'
ⲞⲨⲚ̄ⲦⲀϤ' ⲤⲎⲘⲀⲤⲒⲀ Ⲥ̄ⲚⲦⲈ ⲀⲨΩ ⲠⲈ︤Ⳉ︤Ⲥ̄
ⲀⲨΩ ⲠⲈⲦϢⲎⲨ Ⲓ︤Ⲥ︥ ⳘⲘ̄Ⲛ̄ⳈⲈⲂⲢⲀⲒⲞⲤ ⲠⲈ
ⲠⲤΩⲦⲈ ⲚⲀⳈⲀⲢⲀ ⲦⲈ ⲦⲀⲖⲎⲐⲈⲒⲀ ⲠⲚⲀ

15 ⳈⲀⲢⲎⲚⲞⲤ ⳘⲈ ⲦⲈ ⲦⲀⲖⲎⲐⲈⲒⲀ ⲠⲈ Ⲡ︤Ⳉ︥
Ⲛ̄ⲦⲀⲨϢⲒⲦϤ' ⲠⲚⲀⳈⲀⲢⲎⲚⲞⲤ ⲘⲚ̄ Ⲓ︤Ⲥ︥
ⲚⲈ ⲚⲦⲀⲨϢⲒⲦⲞⲨ ⲠⲘⲀⲢⲄⲀⲢⲒⲦⲎⲤ ⲈⲨϢⲀ̄
ⲚⲞⳈϤ' ⲈⲠⲒⲦⲚ̄ ⲈⲠⲂⲞⲢⲂⲞⲢⲞⲚ ϢⲀϤϢΩ
ⲠⲈ ϢⲀϤϢΩⲠⲈ ⲀⲚ ⲈϤϢⲎⲤ Ⲛ̄ⳈⲞⲨⲞ

[PAGE 64, PLATE 110]

In this Temple Space you become all things,

and you see yourself no more;

and in that All-Other you become all things, and never cease

    to be yourself.

45   Faith [*pistis*] is receiving, and love [*agapē*] is giving.

None can receive without faith,

and none can give without love.

We believe, and are capable of receiving;

we give so as to experience love.

Whoever gives without love experiences nothing of interest.

46   Whoever does not receive the Teacher is still a Hebrew.

47   The apostles before us called him

"Yeshua of Nazareth, the Messiah."

Yeshua first, Messiah last, and Nazareth in between.

Messiah can have two meanings:

"The anointed one"; and "the one who gives limits."

In Hebrew, *Yeshua* means "freedom," and *Nazara* means

    "truth."

Thus the one from Nazareth is the truth, the liberator,

and the giver of limits.

20 ОУТЕ ЕУШАТАЅСЧ · ⲚⲚⲀⲠⲞⲂⲀⲢⲤⲒⲘⲞⲚ
ЕЧⲚⲀⲰⲰⲠⲈ ЕЧⲦⲀⲈⲒⲎⲨ · ⲀⲖⲖⲀ ОУⲚⲦⲀЧ`
ⲘⲘⲀⲨ ⲘⲠⲦⲀⲈⲒⲞ ⲤⲀⲤⲦⲚ ⲠⲈЧ`ϪⲞⲈⲒⲤ`
ОУОЕⲒⲰ ⲚⲒⲘ` ⲦⲀⲈⲒ ⲦⲈ ⲐⲈ ⲚⲚⲰⲎⲢⲈ Ⲙ
ⲠⲚⲞⲨⲦⲈ ⲤⲚ ⲚⲈⲦⲞⲨⲚⲀⲰⲰⲠⲈ ⲚⲤⲎⲦⲞⲨ
25 [Е]ⲦⲒ ОУⲚⲦⲀⲨ ⲘⲘⲀⲨ ⲘⲠⲦⲀⲈⲒⲞ ⲤⲀⲤⲦⲘ ⲠⲞⲨ
ⲈⲒⲰⲦ · ⲈⲔⲰⲀϪⲞⲞⲤ ϪⲈ ⲀⲚⲞⲔ` ОУⲒⲞⲨⲆⲀⲒ
ⲘⲚ ⲖⲀⲀⲨ ⲚⲀⲔⲒⲘ` ⲈⲔⲰⲀϪⲞⲞⲤ` ϪⲈ ⲀⲚⲞⲔ` ОУ
ⲤⲢⲰⲘⲀⲒⲞⲤ Ⲙ.Ⲛ. ⲖⲀⲀⲨ ⲚⲀⲢ̄ⲦⲀⲢⲀⲤⲤⲈ ⲈⲔⲰⲀ
ϪⲞⲞⲤ ϪⲈ ⲀⲚⲞ[Ⲕ О]ⲨⲤ[Е].Ⲗ.ⲖⲎⲚ ОУⲂⲀⲢⲂⲀ
30 .Ⲣ.ⲞⲤ ОУⲤⲘⲌ̄Ⲁ̄Ⲗ̄ [ОУЕⲖⲈⲨ]ⲐⲈⲢⲞⲤ ⲘⲚ ⲖⲀⲀⲨ
ⲚⲀⲰⲦⲞⲢⲦⲢ̄ ⲈⲔ[ⲰⲀϪⲞⲞⲤ] ϪⲈ ⲀⲚⲞⲔ` ОУⲬⲢⲎ
[Ⲥ]ⲦⲒⲀⲚⲞⲤ .Ⲧ.[ⲎⲢⲞⲨ ⲈⲨ]ⲚⲀⲚⲞⲈⲒⲚ ⲚⲄⲈⲚⲞⲒ
[Ⲧ]О ⲚⲦⲀ.Ⲱ.[ⲰⲠ ⲈⲢⲞⲒ ⲘⲠ]ЕЕⲒⲘⲈⲒⲚⲈ ⲠⲀⲈⲒ · Е
[ⲦⲈ ⲚⲀⲢⲬⲰⲚ Ⲛ]ⲀⲰ ⲤⲨⲠⲞⲘⲈⲒⲚⲈ ⲀⲚ · Е
35 [ⲦⲈ ⲠⲀⲒ̈ ⲠⲈ Ⲡ].Е.Ⲓ ⲢⲀⲚ` ⲠⲚⲞⲨⲦⲈ ОУⲀⲘⲢⲰ`

48   A pearl thrown into the mud does not lose its value, and anointing it with oil will not increase its value;

in the eyes of its owner,

its value remains unchanged.

So it is with the sons of God; wherever they are, they are just as precious to their Father.

49   If you say, "I am a Jew," no one will be amazed; if you say, "I am a Roman," no one will be startled; if you say, "I am a Greek, a barbarian, a slave," it will trouble no one. But if you say, "I am a Christian," all will tremble.

Is it possible to bear this name,

when spiritual powers are afraid of it?

50   Humanity is the food of God;

people offer human or animal sacrifices,

but those to whom they sacrifice are not gods.

[PAGE 65, PLATE 111]

ΜΕ ΠΕ ΔΙΑ ΤΟΥΤΟ C[ΕϢΩΩΤ Μ̄]ΠΡΩ[ΜΕ
ΝΑϤ · ϨΑ ΤΕϨΗ ΕΜΠΑΤΟ[Υ]ϢΩΩΤ Μ̄ΠΡΩ
ΜΕ ΝΕΥϢΩΩΤ · Ν̄ϨΝ̄ΘΗΡΙΟΝ ΝΕϨΝ̄ΝΟΥ
ΤΕ ΓΑΡ ΑΝ ΝΕ ΝΑΕΙ ΕΤΟΥϢΩΩΤ · ΝΑΥ
5 Ν̄CΚΕΥΟC Ν̄ΝΑΒΑϬΗΕΙΝ ΜΝ̄ Ν̄CΚΕΥΟC
Β̄ΒΛϪΕ ϢΑΥϢΩΠΕ ΕΒΟΛ ϨΙΤΜ̄ ΠΚΩϨΤ ·
ΑΛΛΑ Ν̄CΚΕΥΟC Ν̄ΝΑΒΑϬΗΕΙΝ ΕΥϢΑ
ΟΥΩϬΠ · ΠΑΛΙΝ ϢΑΥΤΑΜΙΟΟΥ Ν̄ΤΑΥ
ϢΩΠΕ ΓΑΡ ΕΒΟΛ ϨΝ̄ ΟΥΠΝ̄Ᾱ Ν̄CΚΕΥΟC
10 ΔΕ Β̄Β̄Λ̄ϪΕ ΕΥϢΑΟΥΩϬΠ · ϢΑΥΤΑΚΟ
ΝΤΑΥϢΩΠΕ ΓΑΡ ΧΩΡΙC ΝΙϤΕ ΟΥΕΙΩ
ΕϤΚΩΤΕ ϨΑ ΟΥΩΝΕ Ν̄ΝΟΥΤ ΑϤΝ̄ ϢΕ Μ̄ΜΙΛΟC
ΕΒΟΛ ΕϤΜΟΟϢΕ Ν̄ΤΑΡΟΥΚΑΑϤ' ΕΒΟΛ
ΑϤϨΕ ΕΡΟϤ ΟΝ ΕϤϨΜ̄ ΠΙΜΑ ΠΙΜΑ
15 ΟΥΝ ϨϜΡΩΜΕ ϢΟΟΠ · ϢΑΥΝ̄ ϨΑϨ Μ̄ΜΟ
ΟϢΕ · ΕΒΟΛ' ΑΥΩ ΜΑΥΠΡΟΚΟΠΤΕ Ε
ΛΑΑΥ Μ̄ΜΑ Ν̄ΤΑΡΕΡΟΥϨΕ ϢΩΠΕ ΕΡΟ̇
ΟΥ ΟΥΤΕ Μ̄ΠΟΥΝΑΥ ΕΠΟΛΙC ΟΥΤΕ
ΚΩΜΗ ΟΥΤΕ ΚΤΙCΙC ΟΥΤΕ ΦΥCΙC ΜΝ̄

[PAGE 65, PLATE 111]

51   Glass and clay vessels are made with the help of fire.

Glass vessels can be restored, because they are shaped by
breath.

But clay vessels are destroyed when they are broken,

for they were born without breath.

52   A donkey hitched to a mill wheel can travel a hundred miles,
but when you untie him, he is still in the same place. There
are people who walk a great deal, and never get anywhere.

When evening falls, there is nothing to be seen on the
horizon—no village, no creature, no higher power, no
angel to be seen.

Have these people suffered in vain?

53   The work of Yeshua is to render grace [*eukharistia*];

In Syriac, he is called "the one who is spread out,"

for Yeshua came, and the world opened in the four directions
of the cross.

20 ⲆⲨⲚⲀⲘⲓⲤ · ⲘⲚ̄ ⲀⲅⲄⲈⲖⲞⲤ ⲈⲒⲔⲎ ⲀⲚⲦⲀⲖⲀⲒ
ⲠⲰⲢⲞⲤ ⲤⲒⲤⲈ ⲦⲈⲨⲬⲀⲢⲒⲤⲦⲈⲒⲀ ⲠⲈ Ⲓ̄Ⲥ̄ ⲈⲨ
ⲘⲞⲨⲦⲈ ⲄⲀⲢ ⲈⲢⲞϤ Ⲙ̄ⲘⲚ̄ⲦⲤⲨⲢⲞⲤ ⲬⲈ ⲪⲀ
ⲢⲒⲤⲀⲐⲀ ⲈⲦⲈ ⲠⲀⲈⲒ ⲠⲈ ⲠⲈⲦⲠⲞⲢϢ ⲈⲂⲞⲖ
Ⲁ̄Ⲓ̄Ⲥ̄ ⲄⲀⲢ ⲈⲒ ⲈϤⲤⲦⲀⲨⲢⲞⲨ Ⲙ̄ⲠⲔⲞⲤⲘⲞⲤ
25 ⲀⲠⲬⲞⲈⲒⲤ ⲂⲰⲔ ⲈⲤⲞⲨ[Ⲛ] ⲈⲠⲘⲀ Ⲛ̄ⲬⲰϬⲈ
Ⲛ̄ⲖⲈⲨⲈⲒ ⲀϤϤⲒ ϢⲂⲈⲤⲚⲞⲞⲨⲤ Ⲛ̄ⲬⲢⲰⲘⲀ
ⲀϤⲚⲞⲬⲞⲨ ⲀⲦⲢⲞϬⲦⲈ ⲀϤⲚ̄ⲦⲞⲨ ⲈⲤⲢⲀⲒ̈
ⲈⲨⲞⲂϢ ⲦⲎⲢⲞⲨ ⲀⲨⲰ ⲠⲈⲬⲀϤ ⲬⲈ ⲦⲀⲈⲒ
ⲦⲈ ⲐⲈ Ⲛ̄ⲦⲀϤⲈⲒ Ⲙ̄ⲘⲞ‚Ⲛ‚ Ⲛ̄ϬⲒ [Ⲡ]ϢⲎⲢⲈ · Ⲙ̄
30 ⲠϢⲎⲢⲈ Ⲙ̄ⲠⲢⲰ‚Ⲙ‚[Ⲉ ⲈϤⲞ] Ⲛ̄‚ⲬⲒⲦ‚ ⲦⲤⲞ
ⲪⲒⲀ ⲈⲦⲞⲨⲘⲞⲨ[ⲦⲈ ⲈⲢⲞⲤ] ⲬⲈ ⲦⲤⲦⲒ‚Ⲣ‚Ⲁ Ⲛ̄
ⲦⲞⲤ ⲦⲈ ⲦⲘⲀⲀ[Ⲩ Ⲛ̄ⲚⲀⲄⲄ]ⲈⲖⲞⲤ ⲀⲨ‚Ⲱ‚ [Ⲧ]‚ⲔⲞⲒ‚
ⲚⲰⲚⲞⲤ Ⲙ̄Ⲡ‚Ϣ‚[ⲎⲢⲈ ⲦⲈ ⲘⲀⲢ]ⲒⲀ ⲦⲘⲀ‚Ⲅ‚[ⲆⲀ]
ⲖⲎⲚⲎ ⲚⲈⲢⲈⲠ[ⲬⲞⲈⲒⲤ ⲘⲈ] ‚Ⲛ̄‚Ⲙ[ⲀⲢⲒⲀ Ⲛ̄]
35 ⲤⲞⲨⲞ ⲀⲘ̄ⲘⲀⲐⲎ[ⲦⲎⲤ ⲦⲎⲢⲞⲨ ⲀⲨⲰ ⲚⲈϤ]
ⲀⲤⲠⲀⲌⲈ Ⲙ̄ⲘⲞⲤ ⲀⲦⲈ‚Ⲥ‚[ⲦⲀⲠⲢⲞ Ⲛ̄ⲤⲀⲤ]
Ⲛ̄ⲤⲞⲠ · ⲀⲠⲔⲈⲤⲈⲈⲠⲈ ‚Ⲛ‚[Ⲙ̄ⲘⲀⲐⲎⲦⲎⲤ ⲀⲨ]

54 The Teacher went to Levi's dye works;

he took seventy-two colors [*kroma*],

threw them into the vat,

and when he took them out, they were white.

He said: "This is how the Son of Man has come,

like a dyer."

55 The Wisdom [*Sophia*] thought to be sterile [*steira*] is the
mother of angels.

The companion [*koinonos*] of the Son is Miriam of Magdala.

The Teacher loved her more than all the disciples;

he often kissed her on the mouth.

When the disciples saw how he loved Miriam, they asked him:

The Text of the Gospel of Philip

[PAGE 66, PLATE 112]

[ΝΑΥ] ˙Ε˙ΡΟˌϤ ˌ[ΕϤΜΕ ΜΑΡΙ]Α ΠΕΧΑΥ ΝΑϤ ΧΕ
[ΕΤ]ˌΒˌΕ ΟΥ ΚΜˌΕ ΜΜˌΟC ΠΑΡΑΡΟΝ ΤΗΡΝ ΑϤˋ
ΟΥΩϢΒ̄ ΝϬΙ ΠCΩΤΗΡ ΠΕΧΑϤ ΝΑΥ ΠΕ
ΧΑϤ ΝΑΥ ΧΕ ΕΤΒΕ ΟΥ ϮΜΕ ΜΜΩΤΝ ΑΝˋ
5 ΝΤΕCϨΕ ΟΥΒΛΛΕ ΜΝ ΟΥΑ ΕϤΝΑΥ ΕΒΟΛ
ΕΥϨΜ ΠΚΑΚΕ ΜΠΕCΝΑΥ CΕϢΟΒΕ ΕΝΟΥ
ΕΡΗΥ ΑΝ ϨΟΤΑΝ ΕΡϢΑΠΟΥΟΕΙΝ ΕΙˋ ΤΟΤΕ
ΠΕΤΝΑΒΟΛˋ ϤΝΑΝΑΥ ΕΠΟΥΟΕΙΝ ΑΥΩ
ΠΕΤΟ Β̄Β̄Λ̄Ε ΕϤΝΑϬΩ ϨΜ ΠΚΑΚΕ ΠΕ
10 ΧΕ ΠΧΟΕΙC ΧΕ ΟΥΜΑΚΑΡΙΟC ΠΕ ΠΕΤˋϢΟ
ΟΠ ϨΑ ΤΕϨΗ ΕΜˋΠΑΤΕϤˋϢΩΠΕ ΠΕΤϢΟ
ΟΠˋ ΓΑΡ ΑϤϢΩΠΕ ΑΥΩ ϤΝΑϢΩΠΕ ΠΧΙ
CΕ ΜΠΡΩΜΕ ϤΟΥΟΝϨ ΑΝˋ ΕΒΟΛˋ ΑΛΛΑ
ϤϢΟΟΠˋ ϨΜ ΠΕΘΗΠˋ ΕΤΒΕ ΠΑΕΙ ϤΟ Ν̄
15 ΧΟΕΙC ΑΝˋΘΗΡΙΟΝ ΕΤΧΟΟΡ ΕΡΟϤ ΕΤΝΕ
ΑΥ ΚΑΤΑ ΠΕΤΟΥΟΝϨ ΕΒΟΛˋ ΜΝ ΠΕΘΗΠˋ
ΑΥΩ ΠΑΕΙ Ϯ ΝΑΥ ΜΠΜΟΥΝ ΕΒΟΛ ΕΡϢΑ
ΠΡΩΜΕ ΔΕ ΠΩΡΧˋ ΕΡΟΟΥ ϢΑΥΜΟΥΟΥΤˋ
Ν̄ΝΟΥΕΡΗΥ Ν̄CΕΠΩˌϨˌC Ν̄ΝΟΥΕΡΗΥ

[PAGE 66, PLATE 112]

"Why do you love her more than us?"

The Teacher answered:

"How can it be that I do not love you as much as I love her?"

56   When a blind man and one who sees

are both in the dark, there is no difference between them;

but when they both come into the light, one sees it,

and the other remains in darkness.

57   The Teacher said, "Blessed are those who are before existing;

for those who are were, and will be."

58   The superiority of human beings is not apparent, it is a secret;

this is why they can dominate animals who are bigger and

stronger than they in appearance, for it is they who allow

the animals to survive. If humans abandon the animals, they

bite and kill each other.

They eat each other because they lack food.

But now that humans cultivate the earth,

they find food.

20 ΑΥШ ΑΥΟΥШΜ Ñ̄ΝΟΥΕΡΗΥ ϪΕ Μ̄ΠΟΥϨΕ
ΕΤΡΟΦΗ ΤΕΝΟΥ ΔΕ ΑΥϨΕ ΕΤΡΟΦΗ ΕΒΟΛ
ϪΕ ΑΠΡШΜΕ Ρ̄ ϨШΒ ΕΠΚΑϨ ΕΡШΑΟΥΑ'
ΒШΚ' ΕΠΕϹΗΤ ΕΠΜΟΟΥ Ñ̄ΨΕΙ ΕϨΡΑΪ ΕΜ'
ΠΕ ΨϪΙ ΛΑΑΥ Ñ̄ΨϪΟΟϹ ϪΕ ΑΝΟΚ' ΟΥΧΡΗ
25 ϹΤΙΑΝΟϹ Ñ̄ΤΑΨ[ϪΙ] Μ̄ΠΡΑΝ' ΕΤΜΗϹΕ ΕΨ'
ΨϪΙ ΔΕ Μ̄ΠΠ[Ñ̄]Α ΕΤΟΥΑΑΒ ΟΥÑ̄ΤΑΨ Μ̄
ΜΑΥ Ñ̄ΤΔШΡΕΑ Μ̄ΠΡΑΝ ΠΕΝΤΑϨϪΙ Ñ̄ΟΥ
ΔШΡΕΑ ΜΑΥΨΙΤ.Ϲ. Ñ̄ΤΟΟΤΨ' ΠΕΝΤΑϨϪΙ ΔΕ
ΕϪШΨ' ΕΤΜΗϹΕ ΨΑΥΨΑΤΨ' ΤΑΕΙ ΤΕ ΘΕ
30 ΕΤΨ.Ε.[ΛΕΕ]Τ .Ν.[Α].Μ.[Ε Ε].ΡΨ.ΑΟΥΑ ΨШΠΕ ϨÑ̄
ΟΥΜΥϹΤΗΡΙΟ[Ν ΕΤΕ ΠΜΥ]ϹΤΗΡΙΟΝ Μ̄ΠΓΑ
.Μ.[ΟϹ Π].Ε. ΟΥΝΟϬ [ΠΕ ΑϪΝΤ]Ψ̄ ΓΑΡ ΝΕ ΠΚΟϹ
[ΜΟϹ] .Ν.ΑΨШ[ΠΕ ΑΝ ΤϹ].Υ.ϹΤΑϹΙϹ ΓΑΡ' Μ̄
[ΠΚΟϹ]Μ.Ο.[Ϲ ΠΕ ΠΡШ]ΜΕ ΤϹΥϹΤΑϹΙϹ ΔΕ
35 [Μ̄ΠΡШΜΕ ΤΕ ΠΓΑ]ΜΟϹ ΕΡΙΝΟΕΙ Ñ̄ΤΚΟΙ
[ΝШΝΙΑ ΤΑΤϪ].Ω.Ϩ̄Μ̄ ϪΕ ΟΥÑ̄ΤΑϹ Μ̄ΜΑΥ
[ΝΟΥΝΟϬ Ν].Δ.ΥΝΑΜΙϹ ΤΕϹϨΙΚШΝ

59 If someone goes down into the water and emerges without
receiving anything,

and says: "I am a Christian," they usurp the Name.

But if they receive the Breath, they receive the grace of the
Name.

When someone receives a gift [*dorea*] it is not taken from
them.

But if someone takes it for themselves, it will be taken from
them.

60 This is how it is with those united in marriage.

The mystery which unites two beings is great;

without it, the world would not exist.

What gives substance to the world is *Anthropos*.

What gives substance to *Anthropos*

is an intimate and enduring relation [*gamos*]

Seek the experience of the pure embrace [*koinonia*];

it has great power;

contemplate the Presence in this impermanent body.

61 Some of the unclean spirits are masculine, others are feminine.

The masculine ones unite with

souls who inhabit a female form;

the feminine ones mate with

souls who inhabit a male form.

None can be free with respect to these forms unless they receive
a power which is both masculine and feminine.

[PAGE 67, PLATE 113]

ЄСϢООП 2Ñ ОУХ.Ѡ.[2Ñ Ñ].СХ.[НМ]А МП.Ñ.[А]
ÑАКАѲАРТОN ОУÑ .2.О.ОУ.Т Ñ2НТОУ ОУ
Ñ 2ÑС2ІОМЄ Ñ2ООУТ .МЄN. NЄ ЄТР̄КОІ
NѠNЄІ АМΨУХН ЄТР̄ПОЛІТЄУЄСѲЄ

5 2ÑN ОУСХНМА ÑС2ІМЄ ÑС2ІОМЄ ΔЄ
NЄ NЄТТН2 МÑ NЄТ2Ñ ОУСХНМА Ñ
2ООУТ · ЄВОЛ 2ІТÑ ОУАТ.ТѠТ АУѠ МÑ
ЛААУ NАϢ Р̄ ВОЛ ЄNАЄІ ЄУЄМАСТЄ М̄
МОϤ ЄϤТМ̄ХІ ÑОУϬОМ Ñ2ООУТ · МÑ

10 N ОУС2ІМЄ ЄТЄ ПNУМФІОС ПЄ МN
ТNУМФН ОУА ΔЄ ХІ ЄВОЛ 2М̄ ПNУМ'
ФѠN Ñ2ІКОNІКОС 2ОТАN ЄРϢАNС2І
МЄ ÑАТСВѠ NАУ АУ2ООУТ · ЄϤМООС
ОУААϤ ϢАУϤѠϬЄ Є2РАЇ ЄХѠϤ ÑСЄ

15 СѠВЄ NМ̄МАϤ ÑСЄХО2МЄϤ ТЄЄІ2Є
ОN 2Р̄РѠМЄ ÑАТСВѠ ЄУϢАNNАУ ЄУ
С2ІМЄ ЄС2МООС ОУААТС̄ ЄNЄСѠС
ϢАУПІѲЄ М̄МОС ÑСЄР̄ВІАZЄ М̄МОС
ЄУОУѠϢ ЄХО2МЄС ЄУϢАNNАУ ΔЄ

[PAGE 67, PLATE 113]

This is what happens in the bridal chamber

when man and woman become wed.

When immature women see a man sitting alone, they go to

   him, flirt with him, and distract him.

Likewise, when immature men see a pretty woman sitting alone,

they hunger for her, seduce her, and she lets herself be taken.

But if they see a man and a woman seated together,

the women do not chase after the man,

and the men do not chase after the woman.

When the image of God in us is joined to the angel,

no one dares to molest a man or a woman.

20 ΑΠ2ΟΟΥΤ ΜΝ ΤΕΨ2ΙΜΕ ΕΥ2ΜΟΟC 2Α
ΤΝ ΝΟΥΕΡΗΥ ΜΑΡΕΝ2ΙΟΜΕ Ψ ΒΩΚ' Ε
2ΟΥΝ ΨΑ Π2ΟΟΥΤ ΟΥΤΕ ΜΑΡΕΝ2ΟΟΥ.Τ.
Ψ ΒΩΚ' Ε2ΟΥΝ' ΨΑ ΤC2ΙΜΕ ΤΑΕΙ ΤΕ ΘΕ
ΕΡΨΑΘΙΚΩΝ' ΜΝ .Π.[Α]ΓΓΕΛΟC 2ΩΤΡ Ε
25 ΝΟΥΕΡΗΥ ΟΥΤΕ ΜΝ [ΛΑ]ΑΥ ΝΑΨ Ρ̄ΤΟΛΜΑ
ΑΒΩΚ' Ε2ΟΥΝ ΨΑ Φ[Ο].Ο.ΥΤ · Η ΤC2ΙΜΕ
ΠΕΤΝ̄ΝΗΥ ΕΒΟΛ 2[Μ̄] ΠΚΟCΜΟC Ν̄CΕ
ΤΜ̄Ψ ΕΜΑ2ΤΕ Μ̄Μ[ΟΨ]' ΕΤΙ ΧΕ ΝΕΨ2Μ̄
ΠΚΟCΜΟC ΨΟΥΟ[Ν2] ΕΒΟ.Λ. ΧΕ ΨΧΟCΕ
30 ΑΤΕΠΙΘΥΜΙΑ .ΜΠ.[ΜΟ]Υ [ΑΥΩ] .Α.[Τ].2.Ρ̄ΤΕ
ΨΟ Ν̄ΧΟΕΙC Α.Τ.[ΦΥ]CΙC Ψ'CΟ.Τ.Π Ε
ΠΚΩC ΕΨΧ[Ε ΕΥΝΑΥ ΜΠ].Ε.ΕΙ .C.ΕΑ.Μ.[Α].2.ΤΕ
Μ̄ΜΟΨ' CΕΩ.6.[Τ Μ̄ΜΟΨ Α]ΥΩ Π.Ω.[C ΕΨ]
ΝΑΨ Ρ̄ ΒΟΛ ΑΝ.Ι.[ΕΠΙΘΥΜΙ].Α. Μ.Ν̄. [2Ρ]
35 ΤΕ ΠΩC ΨΝΑΨ 2[ΟΠΨ ΕΡΟΟΥ ΠΟΛΛΑ]
ΚΙC ΟΥΝ̄ 2ΟΕΙΝΕ Ε[Ι ΕΥΧΩ Μ̄ΜΟC ΧΕ]
ΑΝΟΝ 2Μ̄ΠΙCΤΟC 2ΟΠ.Ω.[C ΕΨΙ ΕΒΟΛ 2Ν̄]

Whoever is free of the world

can no longer be made into a slave there.

They have risen above attraction and repulsion.

They are master of their nature, free of envy.

If someone sees such a person, they seize them and hold them.

How can one be free of the powers

of attraction and repulsion?

How can they then escape them?

Often there are those who come and say: "We are believers."

They imagine themselves capable of escaping demons and
    unclean spirits.

If they had the Holy Breath in them,

no unclean spirits would adhere to them.

[PAGE 68, PLATE 114]

[M̅Π]N̅A̅ N̅A[ΚΑΘΑΡΤΟΝ] ϨΙ ΔΑΙΜΟΝΙΟΝ˙
ΝΕΥN̅ΤΑΥ ΓΑΡ ˌM̅ˌΜˌΑˌ[Υ] M̅ΠN̅A̅ ΕΤΟΥΑΑΒ
ΝΕΜN̅ ΠN̅A̅ ˌN̅Αˌ ΚΑΘΑΡΤΟΝ ΝΑP̅ΚΟΛΛΑ
ΕΡΟΟΥ ΜN̅P̅ Ϩ ΟΤΕ ϨΗΤC̅ N̅ΤϹΑΡϪ ΟΥΔΕ
5   ΜN̅ΜΕΡΙΤC̅ ΕΚϢΑP̅ ϨΟΤΕ ϨΗΤC̅ ϹΝΑP̅ Ϫ Ο
ΕΙϹ ΕΡΟΚ˙ ΕΚϢΑΝΜΕΡΙΤC̅ ϹΝΑΟΜΚ˙ N̅ϹΟϬΚ
Η N̅ΨϢΩΠΕ ϨΜ̅ ΠΕΕΙΚΟϹΜΟϹ Η ϨN̅ ΤΑΝΑ
ϹΤΑϹΙϹ Η ϨN̅ N̅ΤΟΠΟϹ ΕΤϨN̅ ΤΜΗΤΕ
ΜΗ ΓΕΝΟΙΤΟ N̅ϹΕϨΕ ΕΡΟΕΙ N̅ϨΗΤΟΥ ΠΕ
10   ΕΙΚΟϹΜΟϹ ΟΥM̅ ΠΕΤΝΑΝΟΥ Ϥ N̅ϨΗΤ Ϥ ˙
ΟΥM̅ ΠΕΘΟΟΥ ΝΕ Ϥ ΠΕΤΝΑΝΟΥΟΥ M̅ΠΕ
ΤΝΑΝΟΥΟΥ ΑΝ ΝΕ ΑΥΩ ΝΕ Ϥ ΠΕΘΟΟΥ ϨΜ̅
ΠΕΘΟΟΥ ΑΝ ΝΕ ΟΥN̅ ΠΕΘΟΟΥ ΔΕ ΜN̅N̅
ϹΑ ΠΕΕΙΚΟϹΜΟϹ Ε ϨΜ̅ΠΕΘΟΟΥ ΝΑΜΕ ΝΕ
15   ΤΕΤΟΥΜΟΥΤΕ ΕΡΟϹ ϪΕ ΤΜΕϹΟΤΗϹ N̅ΤΟ Ϥ
ΠΕ ΠΜΟΥ ϨΩϹ ΕΝϢΟΟΠ ϨΜ̅ ΠΕΕΙΚΟϹ
ΜΟϹ ϢϢΕ ΕΡΟΝ ΕϪΠΟ ΝΑΝ N̅ΤΑΝΑϹΤΑ
ϹΙϹ ϪΕΚΑΑϹ ΕΝϢΑΚΑΑΚΝ ΑϨΗΥ N̅ΤϹΑΡϪ
ΕΥΝΑϨΕ ΕΡΟΝ ϨN̅ ΤΑΝΑΠΑΥϹΙϹ N̅ΤN̅ΤM̅

[PAGE 68, PLATE 114]

62 Do not fear the flesh nor be enamored of it.

If you fear it, it will rule you.

If you love it, it will paralyze you and devour you.

63 One is either of the world, or one is resurrected [*anastasis*],

or one is in the intermediate world.

God forbid that I be found there!

In this world there is good and there is evil.

What is good is not all good,

and what is evil is not all evil.

But beyond this world, there is something that is really evil;

it is the intermediate world, the world of the dead.

While we are in this world

it would be right to attain resurrection,

so that, free of the flesh, we know repose [*anapausis*],

and do not become wanderers in the intermediate world.

Many get lost on the way.

It is good to awaken from the world going astray there.

ΜΟΟϢΕ ϨΝ̄ ΤΜΕϹΟΤΗϹ ϨΑϨ ΓΑΡ' ϹΕΡ̄ΠΛΑ
ΝΕϹΘΕ ϨΝ̄ ΤϨΙΗ ΝΑΝΟΥϹ ΓΑΡ ЄЄΙ ЄΒΟΛ
ϨΜ̄ ΠΚΟϹΜΟϹ ϨΑ ΤЄϨΗ ЄΜΠΑΤЄΠΡΩΜЄ
Ρ̄ ΝΟΒЄ ΟΥΝ̄ ϨΟЄΙΝЄ ΜЄΝ ΟΥΤЄ ϹЄΟΥΩϢ
ΑΝ ΟΥΤЄ ΜΝ̄ ϬΟ⸤Μ⸥ ⸤Μ̄⸥ΜΟΟΥ ϨΝ̄ΚΟΟΥЄ ΔЄ
ЄΥϢΑΝΟΥΩϢ [Μ]⸤Μ⸥Ν̄ ϨΗΥ ϢΟΟΠ' ΝΑΥ ϪЄ
Μ̄ΠΟΥЄΙΡЄ Є⸤Τ⸥[ΟΥΟ]ΥΩϢ ΓΑΡ' ϤЄΙΡЄ Μ̄ΜΟ
ΟΥ Ν̄ΡЄϤΡ̄ ΝΟΒЄ [Π]ΤΜ̄ΟΥΩϢ ΔЄ ΤΔΙ
ΚΑΙΟϹΥΝΗ ΝΑϨ[Ω]Π' ЄΡΟΟΥ Μ̄ΠЄϹΝΑΥ
ΑΥΩ ΠΟΥ⸤Ω⸥Ϣ Α⸤Ν⸥ [Μ]Ν̄ ΠЄΙΡЄ ΑΝ · ΟΥΑΠΟ
ϹΤΟΛ⸤ΙΚ⸥[Ο]Ϲ [Ϩ]⸤Ν̄⸥ [ΟΥ]⸤Ο⸥Π⸤Τ⸥ΑϹΙΑ ΑϤΝΑΥ ΑϨΟ
ЄΙΝЄ ЄΥΟ⸤ΤΠ⸥ [Ϩ]Ν̄ ⸤Ο⸥ΥΗЄΙ Ν̄ΚΩϨΤ ΑΥ
Ω ⸤Є⸥[Υ]⸤Μ⸥ΗΡ ϨΝ̄ [ΟΥΗЄΙ] Ν̄ΚΩϨΤ ЄΥΝΗϪ
[ЄΥΗЄ]Ϊ Ν̄ΚΩϨΤ [ЄΥϪΩ ϪΟ]ΟΥ Μ̄ΜΟΟΥ ϨΝ̄
[ΚΩ]⸤Ϩ⸥Τ [............] ⸤Α⸥ΥΩ ΠЄϪΑΥ ΝΑΥ
[ϪЄ.......ΜΝ̄ Ϭ]⸤Ο⸥Μ' Μ̄ΜΟΟΥ ΑΝΟΥϨΜ̄
[Μ̄ΜΟΟΥ.... ΚΑΤΑ] ⸤Μ̄⸥ΠΟΥΟΥΩϢ ΑΥϪΙ
[Μ̄ΠΜΟΥ Ν̄ΟΥ]⸤Κ⸥ΟΛΑϹΙϹ ΠΑЄΙ ЄΤΟΥΜΟΥΤЄ

64   There are some who neither want nor are able to do evil; others want to, but do not. But it is what they want that makes them wicked, and leads them astray, even if they do nothing. Righteousness is lacking in those who want nothing, as in those who do evil.

65   In a vision, the disciple of an apostle
saw several people shut in a house
on fire, and they were attached to it.
"Throw water on the fire," they begged.
They were told that it was impossible to save them.
The outcome of their actions was death.
This is also known as the outer darkness.

66   The soul [*psyche*] and the spirit [*pneuma*] are born of water and
of fire.
It is with water, fire, and light
that the son of the bridal chamber comes into being.
the fire is then an anointing, the fire is then a light.
I do not speak of that fire without form, but of that fire
whose form is white:
a clear light which bestows beauty.

[PAGE 69, PLATE 115]

ЄΡΟϤ ϪЄ ΠΚΑΚЄ ЄΤ[ϨΙΠCΑΝΒΟ].Λ. ϪЄ Ϥ[..]
ЄΒΟΛ ϨΝ ΟΥΜΟΟΥ .ΜΝ. Ο.Υ.ΚΩϨΤ ΝΤΑΤΨ.ΥΧ.[Η]
ΜΝ ΠΠΝΑ ϢΩΠЄ ЄΒΟΛ [ϨΝ] ΟΥΜΟΟΥ ΜΝ
ΟΥΚΩϨΤ · ΜΝΝ ΟΥΟЄΙΝ ΝΤΑΠϢΗΡЄ' Μ

5   ΠΝΥΜΦΩΝ ΠΚΩϨΤ' ΠЄ ΠΧΡΙCΜΑ ΠΟΥΟ
ЄΙΝ ΠЄ ΠΚΩϨΤ' ЄЄΙϢΑϪЄ ΑΝ ΑΠЄЄΙΚΩϨΤ
ЄΤЄ ΜΝΤΑϤ' ΜΟΡΦΗ ΑΛΛΑ ΠΚЄΟΥΑ ЄΤЄϤ
ΜΟΡΦΗ ΟΥΑΒϢ ЄΤΟ ÑΟΥΟЄΙΝ ЄΝЄCΩϤ
ΑΥΩ ЄΤϮ ÑΤΜÑΤCΑ ΤΑΛΗΘЄΙΑ ΜΠЄCЄΙ

10 ЄΠΚΟCΜΟC ЄCΚΑΚ ΑϨΗΥ ΑΛΛΑ ÑΤΑCЄΙ ϨΝ
ÑΤΥΠΟC ΜΝ ÑϨΙΚΩΝ ϤΝΑϪΙΤС ΑΝ' ÑΚЄΡΗ
ΤЄ ΟΥÑ ΟΥϪΠΟ ÑΚЄCΟΠ · ϢΟΟΠ ΜÑΝ ΟΥ
ϨΙΚΩΝ ÑϪΠΟ ÑΚЄCΟΠ' ϢϢЄ ΑΛΗΘΩC
ΑΤΡΟΥϪΠΟΟΥ ÑΚЄCΟΠ · ϨΙΤÑ ΤϨΙΚΩΝ ΑϢ

15 ΤЄ ΤΑΝΑCΤΑCΙC ΑΥΩ ΘΙΚΩΝ ϨΙΤÑ ΘΙΚΩΝ
ϢϢЄ ЄΤΡЄCΤΩΟΥΝ ΠΝΥΜΦΩΝ ΜÑ ΘΙ
ΚΩΝ ϨΙΤÑ ΘΙΚΩΝ ϢϢЄ ЄΤΡΟΥЄΙ ЄϨΟΥΝ
ЄΤΑΛΗΘЄΙΑ ЄΤЄ ΤΑЄΙ ΤЄ ΤΑΠΟΚΑΤΑCΤΑCΙC
ϢϢЄ ΑΝЄΤϪΠΟ ΑΝ ΜΜΑΤЄ ΜΠΡΑΝ' Μ

[PAGE 69, PLATE 115]

67 Truth did not come into the world naked, but veiled with images and archetypes [typos]; otherwise it cannot be received; there is a rebirth through the image of rebirth. One must truly be reborn from this image; this is resurrection.

In passing through the image, the bridegroom is led into the truth

which is the renewal of all things in their integrity [*apocatastasis*].

This is appropriate for those who not only know

the names of Father, Son, and Spirit,

but have integrated them in themselves.

Those who have not integrated these names within themselves

will have their names taken away.

The name of Christian is welcomed with anointing,

in the fullness and energy of the cross,

which the apostles call the union of opposites;

then one is not just Christian, one is the Christ.

20 ΠΕΙΩΤ · ΜΝ ΠϢΗΡΕ ΜΝ ΠΠΝΑ ΕΤΟΥΑΑΒ
ΑΛΛΑ ΑΥϪΠΟΟΥ ΝΑΚ ϨΩΟΥ ΕΤΜΟΥΑ ϪΠ[Ο]
ΟΥ ΝΑϤ· ΠΚΕΡΑΝ ΣΕΝΑϤ[Ι]ΤϤ· ΝΤΟΟΤϤ ·
ΟΥΑ ΔΕ ϪΙ ΜΜΟΟΥ ϨΜ .ΠΧ.ΡΙΣΜΑ ΜΠΣΕ.Ι.
ΝΤΔΥΝΑΜΙΣ · ΜΠΣ.Ϥ.[ΟΣ Ε]Τ.Α.[Ϩ]ΝΕΝΑΠΟΣΤΟ
25 ΛΟΣ ΜΟΥΤΕ ΕΡΟΣ Ϫ[Ε ΤΟ].ΥΝΑ.Μ ΜΝ ΤΕϨΒΟΥ.Ρ.
ΠΑΕΙ ΓΑΡ ΟΥΚΕΤΙ Ο.Υ.[ΧΡΗΣΤΙ]ΑΝΟΣ ΠΕ ΑΛΛ.Α.
ΟΥΧΡ͞Σ ΠΕ ΑΠϪΟΕ[ΙΣ Ρ̄]ϨΩΒ ΝΙΜ · ϨΝΝ ΟΥ
ΜΥΣΤΗΡΙΟΝ ΟΥΒΑ[ΠΤ]ΙΣΜΑ ΜΝ ΟΥΧΡΙΣ
ΜΑ ΜΝΝ ΟΥΕΥΧΑ[ΡΙΣΤΙ].Α. Μ.Ν̄.Ν ΟΥΣΩΤΕ
30 ΜΝΝ ΟΥΝΥΜ.Φ.ΩΝ [ΠϪΟ].ΕΙΣ. [ΠΕϪ]ΑϤ
ΧΕ ΑΕΙ ΕΤΡΑΕ.Ι.[ΡΕ Ν̄ΝΑ ΠΣΑ Μ̄ΠΙΤ]Ν̄ Ν̄
ΘΕ Ν̄ΝΑ ΠΣΑ .Ν̄.[ΤΠΕ ΑΥΩ Ν̄ΝΑ ΠΣΑ Ν̄].Β.ΟΛ
Ν̄ΘΕ Ν̄ΝΑ Π.Σ.[Α Ν̄ϨΟΥΝ ΑΕΙ ΕΤΡΑϨΩΤ]
ΡΟΥ Μ̄ΠΜΑ ΕΤ.Μ.[ΜΑΥ ΑϤΟΥΩΝϨ ΕΒΟΛ Μ̄ΠΑ]
35 ΕΙ ΜΑ ϨΙΤΝ̄ ϨΝ̄ΤΥ[ΠΟΣ ΜΝ ϨΝ̄ΘΙΚΩΝ]
ΝΕΤϪΩ Μ̄ΜΟΣ Ϫ.Ε. [.........]
ΟΥΝ̄ ΟΥΕΙ Μ̄ΠΣΑ Ν̄ΤΠ.Ε. [.... ΕΥΠΛΑ]
ΝΑΣΘΕ ΠΕΤΟΥΟΝϨ .Γ.[ΑΡ ΝΤΕΕΙΜΕ]

68 The Teacher performed all his works mysteriously:

immersing us in water [*baptisma*],

anointing us with oil [*khrisma*],

making us capable of acts of grace [*eukharistia*].

He freed us and brought us into the bridal chamber

[*numphon*].

69 The Teacher said: "I have come to make the lower realities like the higher realities, and the outer realities like the inner realities. I have come to unite them in this Temple Space, where they reveal themselves through images and symbols."

Those who say that there is someone in the sky are mistaken, for He who has appeared has come from the depths, and He who owns the hidden things is beyond all the opposites.

It is right to say that the inner and the outer are one;

what appears to be outside the outer does not exist;

it is the outer darkness.

[PAGE 70, PLATE 116]

[I].N.E ETMMAY .П.[E].TO.[Y]MOYTE EPOЧ' ΧE
ΠЄΤMΠCA M[Π].I.TN ΑΥΩ ΠЄΤЄ ΠЄΘΗΠ'
ΨΟΟΠ · ΝΑЧ ΠЄΤMMAY ΠЄ ЄΤNΤΠЄ M
MOЧ ΝΑΝΟΥC ΓΑΡ NCEΧΟΟC ΧE ΠCA N

5 ZOYN ΑΥΩ ΠЄΤMΠCA ΝΒΟΛ' MN ΠЄΤN
ΠCA ΝΒΟΛ MΠCA ΝΒΟΛ' ЄΤΒЄ ΠΑΪ ΑΠΧΟ
ЄΙC ΜΟΥΤЄ ΑΠΤΑΚΟ ΧE ΠΚΑΚE ЄΤZΙ ΠCA
ΒΟΛ' MN 6E ΨΟΟΠ MΠЄЧΒΑΛ' ΠЄΧΑЧ'
ΧE ΠΑЄΙΩΤ ЄΤZM ΠЄΘΗΠ' ΠЄΧΑЧ ΧE

10 ΒΩΚ' ЄZOYN ЄΠЄΚΤΑΜЄΙΟΝ NΓΨΤΑΜ'
MΠЄΚ'ΡΟ ЄΡΩΚ' NΓΨΛΗΛ' ΑΠЄΚ'ЄΙΩΤ'
ЄΤZM ΠЄΘΗΠ' ЄΤЄ ΠΑЄΙ ΠЄ ΠЄΤZΙ CA
ZOYN MMOOY ΤΗΡΟΥ ΠЄΤZΙ CA ΝZOYN
ΔE MMOOY ΤΗΡΟΥ ΠЄ ΠΠΛΗΡΩΜΑ M

15 MNNCΩЧ' MN 6E MΠЄЧCA ΝZOYN ΠΑ
ЄΙ ΠЄ ЄΤΟΥΨΑΧE ЄΡΟЧ' ΧE ΠЄΤM ΠCA N
ΤΠЄ MMOOY ZΑ ΤЄZΗ MΠЄΧC AZOEINE
ЄΙ ЄΒΟΛ' ЄΒΟΛ ΤΩΝ' ΟΥΚЄΤΙ MΠΟΥΨ'
ΒΩΚ' ЄZOYN ΑΥΩ ΑΥΒΩΚ' ЄΤΩΝ ΟΥΚЄΤΙ

[PAGE 70, PLATE 116]

The Teacher said: "My Father lives in secret."

He has said: "Enter into your chamber, close the door,

and pray to your Father who is there in secret."[42]

This means: in your innermost being.

That which is inside, in the secret of all, is fullness [*pleroma*].

Beyond it is nothing, it contains all.

70   Before Christ, several came forth.

They could no longer return to whence they came,

but neither could they leave the place they entered. Christ came.

    Those who had come in, he brought out;

and those who had gone out, he brought in.

---

42. Cf. Matthew 6:6.

20 ṀⲠⲞⲨϢ Ⲓ ⲈⲂⲞⲖ ⲀϤⲈⲒ ⲆⲈ Ⲛ̄ϬⲒ ⲠⲈⲬⲤ̄ ⲚⲈⲚ
  .Ⲧ.ⲀⲌⲂⲰⲔ' ⲈⲌ[Ⲟ].Ⲩ.Ⲛ' ⲀϤⲚ̄ⲦⲞⲨ ⲈⲂⲞⲖ ⲀⲨⲰ ⲚⲈⲚ
  ⲦⲀⲌⲂⲰⲔ' ⲈⲂ[Ⲟ].Ⲗ.' ⲀϤⲚ̄ⲦⲞⲨ ⲈⲌⲞⲨⲚ Ⲛ̄ⲌⲞⲞⲨ'
  ⲚⲈⲢⲈⲈⲨⲌⲀ [Ⲥ].Ⲛ̄. Ⲁ[ⲆⲀ]Ⲙ' ⲚⲈⲘ̄Ⲛ ⲘⲞⲨ ϢⲞⲞⲠ'
  Ⲛ̄ⲦⲀⲢⲈⲤⲠ.Ⲱ.Ⲣ.Ⲭ. [ⲈⲢ].Ⲟ.Ϥ' ⲀⲠⲘⲞⲨ ϢⲰⲠⲈ ⲠⲀ
25 ⲖⲒⲚ ⲈϤϢⲀ.Ⲃ.[ⲰⲔ ⲈⲌⲞ]ⲨⲚ Ⲛ̄ϤⲬⲒⲦϤ' ⲈⲢⲞϤ ⲘⲚ̄
  ⲘⲞⲨ ⲚⲀϢⲰⲠ.Ⲉ. [Ⲡ].Ⲁ.ⲚⲞⲨⲦⲈ ⲠⲀⲚⲞⲨⲦⲈ Ⲉ
  ⲦⲂⲈ ⲞⲨ ⲠⲬⲞⲈⲒⲤ [Ⲁ].Ⲕ.'ⲔⲀⲀⲦ Ⲛ̄ⲤⲰⲔ' Ⲛ̄ⲦⲀϤⲬⲈ
  ⲚⲀⲈ.Ⲓ. ⲌⲒ ⲠⲤϤⲞⲤ [Ⲛ̄Ⲧ]ⲀϤⲠⲰⲢⲬ' ⲄⲀⲢ' ṀⲠⲘⲀ
  Ⲉ.Ⲧ.[Ṁ].ⲘⲀⲨ. [ⲖⲀⲀ].Ⲩ. .Ⲛ.[ⲒⲘ] Ⲛ̄Ⲧ[Ⲁ]ⲨⲬⲠⲞϤ' ⲈⲂⲞⲖ ⲌṀ
30 ⲠⲈ.Ⲧ.[ⲌⲒⲠⲤⲀⲚ].ⲂⲞ.Ⲗ ⲌⲒⲦṀ ⲠⲚⲞⲨⲦⲈ
  Ⲁ.Ⲡ.[ⲬⲞⲈⲒⲤ ⲦⲰⲞⲨⲚ ⲈⲂ].Ⲟ.Ⲗ ⲌⲚ̄ ⲚⲈⲦⲘⲞⲞⲨⲦ'
  [ⲀϤϢⲰ̄ⲠⲈ Ⲛ̄ⲐⲈ ⲈⲚⲈϤϢ]ⲞⲞⲠ · ⲀⲖⲖⲀ ⲚⲈ
  [ⲢⲈⲠⲈϤⲤⲰⲘⲀ ϢⲞⲞⲠ] ⲈϤⲞ Ⲛ̄ⲦⲈⲖⲈⲒⲞⲚ
  [ⲚⲈⲨⲚ̄ⲦⲀϤ ⲆⲈ ṀⲘⲀⲨ] Ⲛ̄ⲤⲀⲢⲌ ⲀⲖⲖⲀ ⲦⲈⲈⲒ
35 [ⲤⲀⲢⲌ ⲘⲈⲚ ⲞⲨⲤⲀ]ⲢⲌ ⲦⲈ Ⲛ̄ⲀⲖⲎⲐⲈⲒⲚⲎ
  [ⲦⲈⲚⲤⲀⲢⲌ ⲆⲈ] ⲞⲨⲀⲖⲎⲐⲈⲒⲚⲎ ⲀⲚ ⲦⲈ ⲀⲖ
  [ⲖⲀ ⲞⲨⲚ̄ⲦⲀⲚ] Ⲛ̄ⲌⲒⲔⲰⲚ Ⲛ̄ⲦⲀⲖⲎⲐⲈⲒⲚⲎ

71   When Eve was in Adam, there was no death; when she was
      separated from him, death came. If she enters back into
      him, and he accepts her, there will be no more death.

72   "My God, my God, why hast thou forsaken me?"
      The Teacher said these words on the cross,
      for he had gone to the place of separation, so as to reunite
      all that had been separated in God.
      The Teacher rose beyond death.
      He became what he was before the separation.
      His body was whole,
      He had a body, but it was the true body;
      ours is transient,
      an image of our true body.

[PAGE 71, PLATE 117]

ΜΑΡΕΠΑСΤΟС ΨΩ[Π]Ε [Ν]ΝΘΗΡΙΟΝ Ο[Υ]
ΤΕ ΜΑϤϢΩΠΕ ΝΝ2Μ[2ΑΛ] ΟΥΤΕ ΝСΖΙΜΕ
ΕϤΧΟ2Μ ΑΛΛΑ ϢΑϤϢΩΠ[Ε] Ν2ΝΡΩΜΕ
ΝΕΛΕΥΘΕΡΟС ΜΝ 2ΝΠΑΡΘΕΝΟС ΕΒΟΛ
5 2ΙΤΜ ΠΝΑ ΕΤΟΥΑΑΒ СΕΧΠΟ ΜΕΝ ΜΜΟ
ΝΚΕСΟΠ СΕΧΠΟ ΔΕ ΜΜΟΝ 2ΙΤΝ ΠΕ
ΧС 2Μ ΠСΝΑΥ СΕΤΩ2С ΜΜΟΝ 2ΙΤΜ Π
ΠΝΑ ΝΤΑΡΟΥΧΠΟΝ ΑΥ2ΟΤΡΝ ΜΝ ΛΑΑΥ
ΝΑϢ ΝΑΥ ΕΡΟϤ ΟΥΤΕ 2Μ ΜΟΟΥ ΟΥΤΕ 2Ν
10 ΕΙΑΛ ΧΩΡΙС ΟΥΟΕΙΝ ΟΥΤΕ ΠΑΛΙΝ ΚΝΑϢ
ΝΑΥ ΑΝ 2Ν ΟΥΟΕΙΝ ΧΩΡΙС ΜΟΟΥ 2Ι ΑΛ
ΔΙΑ ΤΟΥΤΟ ϢϢΕ ΑΡΒΑΠΤΙΖΕ 2Μ ΠСΝΑΥ
2Μ ΠΟΥΟΕΙΝ ΜΝ ΠΜΟΟΥ ΠΟΥΟΕΙΝ ΔΕ
ΠΕ ΠΧΡΙСΜΑ ΝΕΥΝ ϢΟΜΤ ΝΗΕΙ ΜΜΑ
Ν+ ΠΡΟСΦΟΡΑ 2Ν ΘΙΕΡΟСΟΛΥΜΑ ΠΟΥ
Α ΕϤΟΥΕΝ ΕΠΑΜΝΤΕ ΕΥΜΟΥΤΕ ΕΡΟϤ
ΧΕ ΠΕΤΟΥΑΑΒ ΠΚΕΟΥΑ ΕϤΟΥΗΝ ΕΠСΑ
ΡΗС ΕΥΜΟΥΤΕ ΕΡΟϤ ΧΕ ΠΕΤΟΥΑΑΒ Μ
ΠΕΤΟΥΑΑΒ ΠΜΑ2ϢΟΜΤ ΕϤΟΥΗΝ Α

[PAGE 71, PLATE 117]

73   The bridal chamber

is not for animals, nor for slaves,

nor for the impure;

it is for beings who are free, simple, and silent.

74   It is through the Breath that we come into being, but we are
reborn by the Christ two by two. In his Breath, we
experience a new embrace; we are no longer in duality, but
in unity.

75   None can see themselves in water or in a mirror unless there is
light; none can see themselves in light unless there is a
mirror or water to reflect them.

This is why we must be immersed [*baptizai*] in water and
light;

the light is in the oil of anointment [*khrisma*].

20 ΠΑΕΙΒΤΕ ΕΥΜΟΥΤΕ ΕΡΟϤ ϪΕ ΠΕΤΟΥΑΑΒ
 ̄ΝΝΕΤΟΥΑΑΒ ΠΜΑ ΕϢ.Α.ΡΕΠΑΡΧΙΕΡΕΥ[Ϲ]
ΒⲰΚ' ΕϨΟΥΝ ΕΜΑΥ' ΟΥ.Α.[ΑϤ] ΠΒΑΠΤΙϹΜ[Α]
ΠΕ ΠΗΕΙ ΕΤΟΥΑΑΒ [Π].ϹⲰ.[Τ].Ε. ΠΕΤΟΥΑΑΒ
̄ΜΠΕΤΟΥΑΑΒ ΠΕΤ[ΟΥΑ].Α.[Β] ̄ΝΝΕΤΟΥΑΑΒ
25 ΠΕ ΠΝΥΜΦⲰΝ [ΠΒΑΠΤΙϹ]ΜΑ ΟΥ ̄ΝΤΑϤ
̄ΜΜΑΥ ̄ΝΤΑΝΑϹΤΑϹ[ΙϹ Μ ̄Ν ̄Μ Π]ϹⲰΤΕ ΕΠϹ.Ⲱ.
ΤΕ Ϩ ̄Μ ΠΝΥΜ'ΦⲰΝ [ΕΠΝΥ]ΜΦⲰΝ ΔΕ
Ϩ ̄Μ ΠΕΤϪΟϹΕ ΕΡΟ[ΟΥ........].ΟΟ.[...]
ΚΝΑϨΕ ΑΝ` ΕΤ.Ε.Ϥ [...........].Ⲱ Π.[..]
30 ΝΕ ΝΕΤϢΛΗΛ[................]
ΘΙΕΡΟϹΟΛΥΜ[Α.............. ΘΙΕΡΟ]
ϹΟΛΥΜΑ ΕΥ.Ϣ.[ΛΗΛ.... Ϩ Ν ΘΙΕΡΟϹΟ]
ΛΥΜΑ ΕΥϬⲰ.Ϣ.[Τ.............]
ΝΑΕΙ ΕΤΟΥΜΟΥ[ΤΕ ΕΡΟΟΥ ϪΕ ΝΕΤΟΥ]
35 ΑΑΒ ̄ΝΝΕΤΟΥΑΑ.Β. [............ ΚΑ]
ΤΑΠΕΤΑϹΜΑ ΠⲰϨ .Μ.[ΜΟϤ ΟΥ ΔΕ ΠΕ Π]
ΠΑϹΤΟϹ ΕΙΜΗ ΘΙΚⲰΝ [̄ΜΠΝΥΜΦⲰΝ ΠΕΤ]

76   There were three places of worship in Jerusalem: One was open to the west and was called the Holy; another opened to the south and was called the Holy of holiness; and the third was open to the east and was called the holy of holies, where only the high priest could enter.

Immersion in water and light is the Holy [baptism];

to be free is the Holy of holiness [atonement];

and the holy of holies is the bridal chamber [*numphon*], or communion.

Trust and consciousness in the embrace are exalted above all.

Those who truly pray to Jerusalem

are to be found only in the holy of holies . . .

the bridal chamber.

[PAGE 72, PLATE 118]

[ϨⲘ Ⲡ]ⲤⲀ ⲚⲦ.ⲡ.[ⲉ] .ⲉ.[ⲦⲠⲞⲢⲚ]ⲉⲓ`Ⲁ ⲠⲉϤⲔⲀⲦⲀ
.ⲡ.ⲉⲦⲀⲤⲘⲀ ⲡ.Ⲱ.[Ϩ] .Ⲭ.ⲓⲘ ⲠⲤⲀ ⲚⲦⲠⲉ ϢⲀ
ⲠⲤⲀ ⲘⲠⲒⲦⲚ̄ .Ⲛ.ⲉϢϢⲉ ⲄⲀⲢ ⲉϨⲞⲉⲒⲚⲉ
ⲬⲒⲘ ⲠⲤⲀ ⲘⲠⲒⲦⲚ̄ Ⲛ̄ⲤⲉⲂⲰⲔ` ⲉⲠⲤⲀ Ⲛ`ⲦⲠⲉ
5 ⲚⲉⲚⲦⲀϨ† ϨⲒⲰⲞⲨ Ⲙ̄ⲠⲦⲉⲖⲉⲒⲞⲚ Ⲛ̄ⲞⲨ
ⲞⲉⲒⲚ ⲘⲀⲢⲞⲨⲚⲀⲨ ⲉⲢⲞⲞⲨ Ⲛ̄ϬⲒ Ⲛ̄ⲆⲨⲚⲀ
ⲘⲒⲤ ⲀⲨⲰ ⲘⲀⲨϢ ⲉⲘⲀϨⲦⲉ Ⲙ̄ⲘⲞⲞⲨ ⲞⲨ
Ⲁ Ⲇⲉ ⲚⲀ† ϨⲒⲰⲞϤ` Ⲙ̄ⲠⲒⲞⲨⲞⲉⲒⲚ ϨⲘ
ⲠⲘⲨⲤⲦⲎⲢⲒⲞⲚ ϨⲘ ⲠϨⲰⲦⲢ̄ ⲚⲉⲘ`ⲠⲉⲦ`
10 ⲤϨⲒⲘⲉ ⲠⲰⲢⲬ ⲉⲪⲞⲞⲨⲦ ⲚⲉⲤⲚⲀⲘⲞⲨ
ⲀⲚ Ⲡⲉ ⲘⲚ̄ ⲪⲞⲞⲨⲦ` ⲠⲉϤⲠⲰⲢⲬ Ⲛ̄ⲦⲀϤ
ϢⲰⲠⲉ Ⲛ̄ⲀⲢⲬⲎ Ⲙ̄ⲠⲘⲞⲨ ⲆⲒⲀ ⲦⲞⲨⲦⲞ
ⲀⲠⲉⲬⲢ̄Ⲥ̄ ⲉⲒ ⲬⲉⲔⲀⲀⲤ ⲠⲠⲰⲢⲬ Ⲛ̄ⲦⲀϨ
ϢⲰⲠⲉ ⲬⲒⲚ ϢⲞⲢⲠ` ⲉϤⲚⲀⲤⲉϨⲰϤ ⲉⲢⲀⲦϤ`
15 ⲠⲀⲖⲒⲚ` Ⲛ̄ϤϨⲞⲦⲢⲞⲨ Ⲙ̄ⲠⲤⲚⲀⲨ ⲀⲨⲰ ⲚⲉⲚ
ⲦⲀϨⲘⲞⲨ ϨⲘ ⲠⲠⲰⲢⲬ` ⲉϤⲚⲀ† ⲚⲀⲨ Ⲛ̄ⲞⲨ
ⲰⲚϨ Ⲛ̄ϤϨⲞⲦⲢⲞⲨ ϢⲀⲢⲉⲦⲤϨⲒⲘⲉ Ⲇⲉ
ϨⲰⲦⲢ̄ ⲀⲠⲉⲤϨⲀⲉⲒ ϨⲢⲀⲒ̈ ϨⲘ ⲠⲠⲀⲤⲦⲞⲤ
ⲚⲉⲚⲦⲀϨⲰⲦⲢ̄ Ⲇⲉ ϨⲘ ⲠⲠⲀⲤⲦⲞⲤ ⲞⲨⲔⲉ

[PAGE 72, PLATE 118]

What is the bridal chamber,

if not the place of trust and consciousness in the embrace?

It is an icon of Union,

beyond all forms of possession;

here is where the veil is torn from top to bottom;

here is where some arise and awaken.

77   The powers can do nothing against those who are clothed in
    light;

they cannot see them.

All will be clothed in light

when they enter into the mystery of the sacred embrace.

78   If woman had not been separated from man, she would not die
    with man.

Her separation was at the origin of death.

Christ comes again to heal this wound,

to rediscover the lost unity,

to enliven those who kill themselves in separation,

reviving them in union.

20 ΤΙ ⲤⲈⲚⲀⲠⲰⲢⲬ' ⲆⲒⲀ ⲦⲞⲨⲦⲞ ⲀⲈⲨⲌⲀ
ⲠⲰⲢⲬ ⲀⲀⲆⲀⲘ ⲬⲈ ⲚⲦⲀⳠ⳽ⲰⲦⲢ̄ ⲈⲢⲞⳒ'
ⲀⲚ ⲌⲘ̄ ⲠⲠⲀ.Ⳉ.[ⲦⲞ]Ⳉ ⲦⲮⲨⲬⲎ Ⲛ̄ⲀⲆⲀⲘ' Ⲛ̄
ⲦⲀⳠⲰⲠⲈ [ⲈⲂ]ⲞⲖ ⲌⲚ̄Ⲛ ⲞⲨⲚⲒⳒⲈ ⲠⲈⳉ
ⲌⲰⲦⲢ̄ ⲠⲈ Ⲡ[ⲠⲚ̄].Ⲁ̄ .Ⲡ.[Ⲉ]Ⲛ'ⲦⲀⲨⲦⲀⲀⳒ ⲚⲀⳒ'
25 ⲠⲈ ⲦⲈⳒⲘⲀⲀ[Ⲩ] .ⲀⲨ.[Ⲱ ⲘⲚ̄] ⲦⲈⳒ'ⲮⲨⲬⲎ ⲀⲨ†
ⲚⲀⳒ' Ⲛ̄ⲚⲞ.Ⲩ.[ⲠⲚ̄Ⲁ̄ ⲌⲘ̄] .Ⲡ.ⲈⳉⲘⲀ ⲈⲠⲈⲒ Ⲛ̄
.Ⲧ.ⲀⲢⲈⳒ'ⲌⲰ.ⲦⲢ. [ⲠⲈⲬⲀⳒ'] Ⲛ̄ⲌⲚ̄ⳠⲀⲬⲈ ⲈⲨⲬⲞ
ⳉⲈ ⲀⲚⲆⲨⲚ[ⲀⲘⲒⳉ Ⲁ]ⲨⲢ̄ⲂⲀⳉⲔⲀⲚⲈ ⲈⲢⲞⳒ
[ⲈⲨⲠⲞ].Ⲣ̄Ⲭ. [ⲈⲂⲞⲖ Ⲙ̄ⲠⳌ]ⲰⲦⲢ̄ Ⲙ̄ⲠⲚⲈⲨⲘⲀ
30 [ⲦⲒⲔⲞⳉ Ⲡ].Ⲁ.[Ⲭ̄ Ⲛ̄ ⲦⲔⲀ].ⲔⲒⲀ.ⲦⲈⲐⲎⲠ' ⲀⲨ
[............ Ⲗ].Ⲁ.ⲈⲒⳆⲈ Ⲛ̄ⳒⲒ ⲠⲈ
[...............].Ⳉ.ⲚⲀⲨ ⲞⲨⲀⲀⲨ
[............ Ⲙ̄ⲠⲠⲀ]ⳉⲦⲞⳉ ⳠⲒⲚⲀ
[Ⲛ̄ⲢⲰⲘⲈ ⲈⲨⲚⲀⲌⲞⲦⲢ]ⲞⲨ ⲀⲒ⳼ ⳠⲰⲖⲠ'
35 [ⲈⲂⲞⲖ ⲌⲒ ⲘⲎⲢ Ⲙ̄ⲠⲈⲒⲞ]Ⲣ̄ⲆⲀⲚⲎⳉ ⲠⲠⲖⲎ
[ⲢⲰⲘⲀ Ⲛ̄ⲦⲘⲚ̄ⲦⲢ̄].Ⲣ.Ⲟ Ⲛ̄Ⲙ̄ⲠⲎⲨⲈ ⲠⲈ̄
[ⲦⲀⳠⲰⲠⲈ Ⲍ]Ⲁ ⲦⲈⳌⲎ Ⲙ̄ⲠⲦⲎⲢⳒ ⲠⲀ'

79 Man and woman unite in the bridal chamber, and those who
have known this sacred embrace will never be separated.
Eve separated from Adam because she did not unite with
him in the bridal chamber.

80 Adam's soul is animated by the Breath;

it came to him from his mother.

When his soul and his spirit were reunited,

he spoke words that the powers cannot understand.

They were jealous of him, because they were incapable of

this spiritual union which has no hidden violence.

81 On the banks of the Jordan, Yeshua manifested

the Presence of a realm that existed before all things.

[PAGE 73, PLATE 119]

ΛΙΝ ΑΥϪΠΟϤ· Π[ΑΛΙΝ ΑΥϪΠ]ΟϤ ⲚϢΗ.Ρ.[Ε]
ΠΑΛΙΝ ΑΥΤΟ2ϹϤ .Π.[ΑΛΙΝ] ΑΥϹΟΤϤ ΠΑ
ΛΙΝ ΑϤϹⲰΤΕ ΕϢϪΕ .Ϣ.ϢΕ ΕϪⲰ ⲚΟΥ
ⲘΥϹΤΗΡΙΟΝ ΑΠΕΙⲰΤ ⲘΠΤΗΡϤ· 2ⲰΤⲢ̄
5 ΑΤ·ΠΑΡΘΕΝΟϹ ⲚΤΑ2ΕΙ ΑΠΙΤⲚ ΑΥⲰ
ΑΥΚⲰΤ· Ρ̄ ΟΥΟΕΙΝ ΕΡΟϤ ⲘϤΟΟΥ ΕΤⲘ
ΜΑΥ ΑϤϬⲰΛΠ· ΕΒΟΛ ⲘΠΝΟϬ ⲘΠΑϹΤΟϹ
ΕΤΒΕ ΠΑΕΙ ΠΕϤϹⲰΜΑ ⲚΤΑϤϢⲰΠΕ
ⲘϤΟΟΥ ΕΤⲘΜΑΥ ΑϤΕΙ ΕΒΟΛ 2Μ ΠΠΑ
10 ϹΤΟϹ ⲚΘΕ ⲘΠΕΝΤΑ2ϢⲰΠΕ ΕΒΟΛ
2Μ̄ ΠΝΥΜΦΙΟϹ ΜⲚ ΤΝΥΜΦΗ ΤΑ
ΕΙ ΤΕ ΘΕ ΑΪϹ ΤΕ2Ο ⲘΠΤΗΡϤ· ΕΡΑΤϤ·
2ΡΑΪ Ⲛ2ΗΤϤ· ΕΒΟΛ 2ΙΤⲚ ΝΑΕΙ ΑΥⲰ
ϢϢΕ ΕΤΡΕΠΟΥΑ ΠΟΥΑ ⲚⲘΜΑΘΗΤΗϹ
15 ΜΟΟϢΕ Ε2ΟΥΝ ΕΤΕϤ·ΑΝΑΠΑΥϹΙϹ
ΑΑΔΑΜ ϢⲰΠΕ ΕΒΟΛ 2Ⲛ ΠΑΡΘΕΝΟϹ
ϹⲚΤΕ ΕΒΟΛ 2Μ̄ ΠΠⲚᾹ Α.Υ.Ⲱ ΕΒΟΛ·
2Μ̄ ΠΚΑ2 ⲘΠΑΡΘΕΝΟϹ ΕΤΒΕ ΠΑΕΙ
ΑΥϪΠΕ ΠΕΧ̄Ϲ̄ ΕΒΟΛ 2Ⲛ ΟΥΠΑΡΘΕΝΟ[Ϲ]

[PAGE 73, PLATE 119]

In this new generation he manifests as the Son,

then he is anointed.

A free man who was a liberator.

82   Is it permitted to speak what is hidden?

The Father of all that is united with the Silence

of woman, and he illumined it.

He manifested in the bridal chamber;

his body was born on that day when he was witness to the

   Union,

fruit of the merging of the Lover and the Beloved.

This is how Yeshua grounds his disciples in repose.

He is the harmony in all.

20 ϪⲈⲔⲀⲀⲤ ⲠⲈⲤⲖⲞⲞⲦⲈ ⲚⲦⲀϨϢⲰⲠⲈ
ϨⲚ ⲦⲈϨⲞⲨⲈⲓⲦⲈ ⲈϤⲚ.Ⲁ.[Ⲥ].Ⲉ.ϨⲞϤ ⲈⲢⲀⲦϤ
ⲞⲨⲚ ϢⲎⲚ ⲤⲚ[ⲀⲨ Ϩ].Ⲛ. Ⲧ[ⲘⲎⲦ].Ⲉ. ⲘⲠⲠⲀⲢⲀⲆⲒ
ⲤⲞⲤ ⲠⲞⲨⲀ ϪⲠⲈ [ⲐⲎⲢⲒⲞⲚ] ⲠⲞⲨⲀ ϪⲠⲈ
ⲢⲰⲘⲈ ⲀⲀⲆⲀⲘ .Ⲟ.[ⲨⲰⲘ Ⲉ]ⲂⲞⲖ ϨⲘ ⲠϢ.Ⲏ.[Ⲛ]
25 ⲚⲦⲀϨϪⲠⲈ ⲐⲎⲢⲒ[ⲞⲚ ⲀϤϢ].ⲰⲠ.Ⲉ ⲚⲐⲎ
ⲢⲒⲞⲚ ⲀϤϪⲠⲈ Ⲑ.Ⲏ.[ⲢⲒⲞⲚ Ⲉ]Ⲧ.Ⲃ.Ⲉ ⲠⲀⲒ̈ ⲤⲈ
Ⲣ̄ⲤⲈⲂⲈⲤⲐⲈ ⲀⲚ.Ⲑ.[ⲎⲢⲒⲞⲚ ⲈⲨⲞ] Ⲛ̄[ⲦⲈⲒϨⲈ]
Ⲛ̄ⲀⲆⲀⲘ ⲠϢⲎ[Ⲛ ⲚⲦⲀϤⲀⲆⲀⲘ ⲞⲨⲰⲘ ⲘⲠⲈϤ]
ⲔⲀⲢⲠⲞⲤ ⲠⲈ [ⲠϢⲎⲚ Ⲛ̄Ⲛ̄ⲐⲎⲢⲒⲞⲚ ⲈⲦⲂⲈ]
30 ⲠⲀⲈⲒ ⲀⲨⲀ.Ϣ.[Ⲱ ⲚⲈϤϢⲎⲢⲈ Ⲛ̄ⲦⲀⲨ]
ⲞⲨⲰⲘ ⲘⲠ[ⲔⲀⲢⲠⲞⲤ ⲘⲠϢⲎⲚ Ⲛ̄ⲚⲐⲎⲢⲒⲞⲚ]
ⲔⲀⲢⲠⲞⲤ Ⲙ̄.Ⲡ.[ϢⲎⲚ Ⲛ̄ⲚⲐⲎⲢⲒⲞⲚ ⲀϤ]
ϪⲠⲈ Ⲛ̄Ⲣ̄Ⲣ̄ⲰⲘ[Ⲉ ⲚⲐⲎⲢⲒⲞⲚ ⲈⲦⲈ ⲞⲨⲰ]
Ϣ̄Ⲧʼ Ⲙ̄ⲠⲢⲰⲘⲈ [ⲚⲐⲎⲢⲒⲞⲚ Ⲁ.Ⲩ.Ⲱ Ⲁ]
35 ⲠⲚⲞⲨⲦⲈ ⲦⲀⲘⲈⲒⲈ ⲠⲢ[ⲰⲘⲈ ⲀⲨⲰ ⲀⲚⲢⲰ]

83   Adam was born of two virgins; the breath and the earth.

The Logos is born of silence,

to witness that the origin of humanity

was not simply a fall.

84   There are two trees in the middle of the garden [*paradeisos*]:

One engenders animals, the other engenders humans.

Adam ate from the tree that engenders animals,

and became animal.

It is good to revere animals,

for they are like the first human.

The tree from which Adam ate was the tree of animals,

and it bore many fruits.

There is no lack of animal-humans,

they are many, and they revere each other.

In the beginning, God created humans;

then humans created gods.

[PAGE 74, PLATE 120]

ΜΕ ΤΑΜΕ.Ι.[Ε] Π[Ν].ΟΥ.[Τ]Ε ΤΑΕΙ ΤΕ ΘΕ ΖΜ ΠΚΟϹ
ΜΟϹ ΕΝΡΩ[ΜΕ] .Τ.ΑΜΙΕ ΝΟΥΤΕ ΑΥΩ ϹΕΟΥ
ΩΥΤ Ν̄Ν[Ο]ΥΤΑΜΙΟ ΝΕΥΥΕ ΕΤΡΕΝ̄ΝΟΥ
ΤΕ ΟΥΩΥΤ' Ν̄Ρ̄ΡΩΜΕ Ν̄ΘΕ ΕϹΥΟΟΠ' Μ̄
5   ΜΟϹ Ν̄ϬΙ ΤΑΛΗΘΕΙΑ Ν̄Ν̄ΖΒΗΥΕ Μ̄ΠΡΩ
ΜΕ ΥΑΥΥΩΠΕ ΕΒΟΛ ΖΝ̄ ΤΕϤ'ΔΥΝΑΜΙϹ
ΕΤΒΕ ΠΑΕΙ ϹΕΜΟΥΤΕ ΕΡΟΟΥ ΧΕ Ν̄ΔΥ
ΝΑΜΙϹ ΝΕϤΖΒΗΥΕ ΝΕ ΝΕϤ'ΥΗΡΕ Ν̄ΤΑΥ
ΥΩΠΕ ΕΒΟΛ ΖΝ̄ ΟΥΑΝΑΠΑΥϹΙϹ ΕΤΒΕ
10 ΠΑΕΙ ΤΕϤΔΥΝΑΜΙϹ Ρ̄ΠΟΛΙΤΕΥΕϹΘΕ
ΖΡΑΪ ΖΝ̄ ΝΕϤΖΒΗΥΕ ΕΤΑΝΑΠΑΥϹΙϹ ΔΕ
ΟΥΟΝΖ ΕΒΟΛ ΖΡΑΪ ΖΝ̄ Ν̄ΥΗΡΕ ΑΥΩ`
ΚΝΑΖΕ ΕΠΑΕΙ · ΕϤΧΩΤΕ ΥΑ ΖΡΑΪ ΕΘΙΚΩ̄
ΑΥΩ ΠΑΕΙ ΠΕ ΠΡΩΜΕ Ν̄ΖΙΚΟΝΙΚΟϹ

[PAGE 74, PLATE 120]

85   This is the way of the world: Humans create gods

and worship their creations;

now their creations may revere them,

and gods worship humans.

86   The works of humans come from their power; this is why they

are called energies [*dunamis*]. Their children are born from

their repose [*anapausis*];

their power is manifested in their works,

and their repose in their children.

This is an image—humans produce their works with effort,

and their children in repose.

15 ЄЧЄІРЄ ⲚⲚЄЧ2ВНҮЄ ЄВОⲖ 2Ⲛ ТЄЧ6ОМ
ЄВОⲖ ⲆЄ 2Ⲛ ⲀⲚⲀⲠⲀҮⲤⲒⲤ ЄЧⲬⲠⲞ ⲚⲚЄЧˈ
ϢНРЄ 2Ⲙ ⲠЄЄІКОⲤМОⲤ ⲚⲞⲘ̄2Ⲁ̄Ⲗ̄ Ⲣ̄
2ҮⲠНРЄТЄІ ⲚЄⲖЄҮⲐЄРОⲤ 2Ⲛ ТМⲚ
ТЄРО ⲚⲘ̣.Ⲡ̣ⲎⲨЄ ⲚЄⲖЄҮⲐЄРОⲤ ⲚⲀⲢ̄

20 ⲆⲒⲀⲔⲞⲚ[ЄⲒ] ⲚⲚ2Ⲙ̄2Ⲁ̄Ⲗ̄ ⲚⲚ̄ϢНРЄ Ⲙ
ⲠⲚҮМФ[ⲰⲚ ⲚⲀ]Ⲣ̄ⲆⲒⲀⲔⲞⲚЄⲒ ⲚⲚ̄ϢН
РЄ ⲘⲠⲄⲀ[МОⲤ Ⲛ̄]ϢНРЄ ⲘⲠⲚҮМФⲰⲚ
ˌⲞˌҮРⲀⲚ Ⲟ[ҮⲀ ⲠЄ Є]ТЄ ОҮⲚТⲀҮЧ ТⲀⲚⲀ
ⲠⲀҮⲤⲒⲤ Є[ⲤⲘⲚ Ⲛ]ОҮЄРНҮ ⲤЄⲢ̄ ХРЄⲒⲀ ⲀⲚ

25 [...]Ⲣ̄[........] ТЄⲐЄⲰРЄⲒⲀ ⲘⲘⲀҮ
[......... ⲰФЄⲖ]НⲤⲒⲤ 2Ⲛ̄2ОҮО ⲚЄ
[......... ⲐЄⲰР]ˌЄˌⲒⲀ 2Ⲛ ⲚЄТ2Ⲛ̄ Ⲡˈ
[............]Ⲛ̄ⲚЄООҮ ⲚⲚЄ
[............] ⲘⲘОҮ ⲀⲚ ⲚЄ

30 [.... ⲚТⲀⲠⲬ̄Ⲥ̄ В]ⲰКˈ ЄⲠⲒТⲚ̄ ЄⲠМО
[ОҮ ХЄ ЄЧⲚⲀⲬⲞⲔⲞҮ] ЄВОⲖˈ ЄЧⲚⲀⲤОТЧˈ
[ОҮ Ⲛ̄ТⲀРОҮⲬⲎ]Кˈ ЄВОⲖ Ⲛ̄6І ⲚЄⲚ̄ТⲀ2
[ⲬⲞⲔОҮ ЄВОⲖ] 2Ⲙ ⲠЄЧРⲀⲚ ⲠЄⲬⲀЧ ⲄⲀР
[ϢϢЄ ЄРОⲚ] ˌЄˌⲚⲀⲬⲰК ЄВОⲖ Ⲛ̄ⲆⲒⲔˌⲀˌ[Ⲓ]

87 In this world slaves serve those who are free; in the kingdom of heaven those who are free will serve slaves; those who are born in the bridal chamber are in repose. They need nothing else; contemplation suffices them.

88 In this contemplation they dwell among the bodies of glory.

89 Christ immerses them in water to purify them and leads them to their fulfillment in his Name. He said: "It is befitting to fulfill all justice."[43]

---

43. Cf. Matthew 3:15.

[PAGE 75, PLATE 121]

ΟⲨΝΗ ΝΙΜ' ΝΕΤ[Ⲭ]Ⲱ [Ⲙ].Ⲙ.ⲞⲤ Ⲭⲉ ⲤⲈΝΑ
ΜΟⲨ Ⲛ̄ⲰⲞⲢⲠ' ΑⲨⲰ ⲤⲈ.Ⲛ.[ΑⲦ]ⲰⲞⲨΝ ⲤⲈ
Ⲣ̄ⲠⲖΑΝΑⲤ⳿ΘⲈ ⲈⲨⲦⲘ̄Ⲭⲓ Ⲛ̄ⲰⲞⲢⲠ' Ⲛ̄ⲦΑΝΑ
ⲤⲦΑⲤⲓⲤ ⲈⲨⲞΝⲊ ⲈⲨ⳿ⲰΑΜΟⲨ ⲤⲈΝΑⲬⲓ ⲖΑ
5 ΑⲨ ΑΝ ⲦΑⲈⲓ ⲦⲈ ΘⲈ ΟΝ ⲈⲨⲬⲰ Ⲙ̄ΜΟⲤ Ⲉ
ⲠΒΑⲠⲦⲓⲤ⳿ΜΑ ⲈⲨⲬⲰ ΜΜΟⲤ Ⲭⲉ ΟⲨΝΟⳆ
ⲠⲈ ⲠΒΑⲠⲦⲓⲤ⳿ΜΑ Ⲭⲉ ⲈⲨ⳿ⲰΑⲬⲓⲦⳆ' ⲤⲈΝΑ
ⲰΝⲊ ΦⲓⲖⲓⲠⲠⲞⲤ ⲠΑⲠⲞⲤⲦⲞⲖΟⲤ ⲠⲈ
ⲬΑⳆ Ⲭⲉ Ⲓ̄ⲰⲤΗⲪ' Ⲡ̄ⲊΑΜⲰⲈ ΑⳆⲦⲰⳆⲈ Ⲛ̄
10 ΝΟⲨⲠΑⲢΑⲆⲈⲓⲤⲞⲤ Ⲭⲉ ΝⲈⳆⲢ̄ ⲬⲢⲈⲓΑ Ⲛ̄ⲊⲚ̄
ⲰⲈ ⲈⲊΟⲨΝ' ⲈⲦⲈⳆ'ⲦⲈⲬΝΗ Ⲛ̄ⲦΟⳆ ⲠⲈΝ
ⲦΑⲊⲦΑΜⲓⲞ Ⲙ̄ⲠⲤⲦΑⲨⲢΟⲤ ⲈΒΟⲖ ⲊⲚ̄ Ⲛ̄
ⲰΗΝ Ⲛ̄ⲦΑⳆⲦΟⳆΟⲨ ΑⲨⲰ ⲠⲈⳆⳆⲢΟⳆ ΝⲈⳆ
ΟⲨⲰⲈ ΑⲠⲈΝⲦΑⳆⲦΟⳆⳆ' ΝⲈⲠⲈⳆⳆⲢΟⳆ ⲠⲈ
15 Ⲓ̄Ⲏ̄Ⲥ̄ ⲠⲦⲰⳆⲈ ⲆⲈ ⲠⲈ ⲠⲈⲤⳆⲞⲤ ΑⲖⲖΑ ⲠⲰⲚ̄
Ⲙ̄ⲠⲰΝⲊ ⲊⲚ̄ ⲦΜΗⲦⲈ Ⲙ̄ⲠⲠΑⲢΑⲆⲈⲓⲤⲞⲤ
ΑⲨⲰ ⲦΒⲈ Ⲛ̄ⲬΟⲈⲓⲦ' Ⲛ̄ⲦΑⲠⲈⲬⲢⲈⲓⲤⲘΑ ⲰⲰ
ⲠⲈ ⲈΒΟⲖ' Ⲛ̄ⲊΗⲦ̄Ⲥ̄ ⲈΒΟⲖ ⲊⲓⲦΟΟⲦⳆ' ΑⲦΑ
ΝΑⲤⲦΑⲤⲓⲤ (ⲰⲰⲠⲈ) ⲠⲈⲈⲓⲔⲞⲤⲘΟⲤ ΟⲨΑΜⲔⲰ

[PAGE 75, PLATE 121]

90   Those who say that we first die, and then are resurrected, are
wrong.

Whoever is not resurrected before death

knows nothing, and will die.

Thus those who have received baptism will live;

baptism is a great thing.

91   The apostle Philip relates that Joseph the carpenter

planted trees in his garden,

because he needed wood for his work.

The cross was made with the trees he planted,

and the fruit of his seed was hung from the wood that he had
planted.

His seed was Yeshua, and the cross was the plant.

92   The tree of life lives in the middle of another garden; it is the
olive tree from which the oil of anointment is drawn.

Thanks to it, resurrection is possible.

20 ⲰⲤ ⲠⲈ ⲚⲔⲈ ⲚⲒⲘˈ ⲈⲦⲞⲨⲰⲘˈ ⲘⲘⲞⲞⲨ
ⲤⲢⲀⲒ ⲚⲌⲎⲦϤ · ⲤⲈⲘⲈ[Ⲥ]Ⲧ.Ⲱ.Ⲟ.Y ⲞⲚˈ ⲦⲀⲖⲎⲐⲈ.Ⲓ,
Ⲁ ⲞⲨⲀⲘⲰⲚⲌ ⲦⲈ Ⲉ.Ⲧ.[ⲂⲈ] Ⲡ[ⲀⲈ]ⲈⲒ ⲘⲚ ⲖⲀⲀⲨ
ⲌⲚ ⲚⲈⲦⲤⲞⲚⲮ Ⲍ.Ⲛ, [ⲦⲘⲈ ⲚⲀ]ⲘⲞⲨ ⲚⲦⲀˈⲒⲤ̄
ⲈⲒ ⲈⲂⲞⲖ ⲌⲘ̄ ⲠⲘⲀ [ⲈⲦⲘ̄].Ⲙ.[Ⲁ].Y. ⲀⲨⲰ ⲀϤⲈⲒ
25 ⲚⲈ Ⲛ̄ⲌⲚ̄ⲦⲢⲞⲪⲎ Ⲉ.Ⲃ.[Ⲟ].Ⲗ, Ⲙ̄ⲘⲀⲨ ⲀⲨⲰ ⲚⲈ
ⲦⲞⲨⲰⲮ ⲀϤϮ ⲚⲀⲨ [Ⲙ̄Ⲡ].Ⲱ.[ⲚⲌ] .Ⳉ.[ⲈⲔⲀⲀⲤ]
Ⲛ̄ⲚⲞⲨⲘⲞⲨ ⲀⲠⲚ[ⲞⲨⲦⲈ ⲦⲀ].ⲘⲒⲈ, Ⲛ̄[ⲞⲨⲠⲀⲢⲀ]
ⲆⲈⲒⲤⲞⲤ ⲀⲠⲢ.Ⲱ.[ⲘⲈ ⲰⲚⲌ ⲌⲘ̄ ⲠⲀⲢⲀ]
ⲆⲈⲒⲤⲞⲤ ⲞⲨⲚ̄[............ Ⲯⲟ]
30 ⲞⲠ ⲘⲚ ⲌⲘ̄Ⲡ[.................]
Ⲙ̄ⲠⲚⲞⲨⲦⲈ Ⲍ.Ⲛ̄.[.......... ⲢⲰ]
ⲘⲈ ⲚⲈⲦⲚ̄ⲌⲎⲦ[Ϥ.........]
Ϯ ⲞⲨⲰⲮ ⲠⲒⲠⲀⲢⲀ[ⲆⲈⲒⲤⲞⲤ ⲠⲈ ⲠⲘⲀ Ⲉ]
ⲦⲞⲨⲚⲀⳈⲞⲞⲤ ⲚⲀⲈⲒ Ⳉ[Ⲉ ⲞⲨⲰⲘ ⲈⲂⲞⲖ Ⲍ]
35 Ⲙ̄ⲠⲀⲈⲒ Ⲏ Ⲙ̄ⲚⲞⲨⲰⲘ [Ⲙ̄ⲠⲀⲈⲒ Ⲛ̄ⲐⲈ ⲈⲔ]

93   This world is an eater of corpses.

Everything eaten here has the taste of hatred;

the truth is fed by that which is alive,

and those who feed on truth are alive.

Yeshua comes from that Space,

and he gives this food to those who desire it.

They will not die.

94   God planted trees in a garden.

Humans lived among these trees,

they were not yet divided when they were told:

"Eat from this tree, or do not eat from it."

ΟΥΩϢ ΠΑΕΪ Π.ΜΑ Ε. ϮΝΑΟΥΩΜˈ ⲚКЕ ΝΙΜ
ΜΜΑΥ ΕϤϢ.Ο.[ΟΠ] ΜΜΑΥ ⲚϬΙ ΠϢΗΝ ⲚΤˈ
ΓΝΩCΙC Π.Ε.ΤⲘΜΑΥ ΑϤΜΟΥΤˈ ΑΔΑΜ ΠΕ
ΕΙΜΑ ΔΕ ΠϢΗΝ ⲚΤΓΝΩCΙC ΑϤⲚϨΕ ΠΡΩ

5 ΜΈ ΠΝΟΜΟC ΝΕΠϢΗΝ ΠΕ ΟΥⲚ ϬΟΜ
ΜΜΟϤ Ⲛϥ Ϯ ΤΓΝΩCΙC ⲘΠΠΕΤΝΑΝΟΥϤˈ
ⲘⲚ ΠΕΘΟΟΥ ΟΥΤΕ ⲘΠΕϤⲖΑϬΕ ΕΡΟϤ ϨⲘ
ΠΠΕΘΟΟΥ ΟΥΤΕ ⲘΠΕϤˈΚΑΑϤ ϨⲘ ΠΠΕΤΝΑ
ΝΟΥϤ ΑⲖⲖΑ ΑϤΤΑΜΙΟ Ⲛ ΟΥΜΟΥ ⲚΝΕΝΤΑϨ

10 ΟΥΩΜˈ ΕΒΟⲖ Ⲛ ϨΗΤϤˈ ϨⲘ ΠΤΡΕϤ ϪΟΟC ΓΑΡ
ϪΕ ΟΥΩΜˈ ΠΑΕΙ · ⲘⲚΟΥΩΜˈ ΠΑΕΙ ΑϤ Ϣ Ω
ΠΕ Ⲛ ΑΡΧΗˈ ⲘΠΜΟΥ ΠΧΡΕΙCΜΑ ϤΟ Ⲛ ϪΟ
ΕΙC ΕΠΒΑΠΤΙCΜΑ ΕΒΟⲖ ΓΑΡ ϨⲘ ΠΧΡΙCΜΑ
ΑΥΜΟΥΤΕ ΕΡΟΝ · ϪΕ ΧΡΙCΤΙΑΝΟC ΕΤΒΕ

15 ΠΒΑΠΤΙCΜΑ ΑΝ · ΑΥΩ Ⲛ ΤΑΥΜΟΥΤΕ ΕΠΕ
Χ̅C̅ ΕΤΒΕ ΠΧΡΙCΜΑ ΑΠΕΙΩΤˈ ΓΑΡ · ΤΩϨC
ⲘΠϢΗΡΕ ΑΠϢΗΡΕ ΔΕ ΤΩϨC Ⲛ ΑΠΟCΤΟ
ⲖΟC ΑΝΑΠΟCΤΟⲖΟC ΔΕ ΤΑϨCⲚ ΠΕΝ
ΤΑΥΤΟϨCϤˈ ΟΥ Ⲛ ΤΕϤˈ ΠΤΗΡϤˈ ⲘΜΑΥ ΟΥⲚ

[PAGE 76, PLATE 122]

The tree of the knowledge of happiness and unhappiness
killed Adam;

but the tree of true knowledge, the tree of life,

enlivens humankind.

The law [*nomos*] is a tree which separates good and evil;

happiness and unhappiness offer nothing beyond.

It is not for humans to avoid evil, nor establish themselves in
good.

When it was said: "Eat this, and do not eat that,"

that was the origin of their death.

95 To be anointed with oil is higher than being immersed in
water.

It is when we are anointed, not when we are immersed in water,

that we become Christians.

Christ was called *Messiah* because of this:

he is "the anointed one."

20 ΤΑϤ ΤΑΝΑCΤΑCΙC ΠΟΥΟΕΙΝ ΠΕCϤΟC˙
ΠΠΝ͞Α ΕΤΟΥΑΑΒ ΑΠΕΙΩΤ ϯ ΝΑϤ Μ͞ΠΑ
ΕΙ Ζ͞Μ ΠΝΥ[Μ]Φ˴Ω˴[Ν] ΑϤΧΙ ΑϤϢΩΠΕ Ν͞ϬΙ
ΠΕΙΩΤ˙ Ζ˴Μ͞ ΠϢ˴[ΗΡ]Ε ΑΥΩ ΠϢΗΡΕ Ζ͞Μ ΠΕΙ
ΩΤ˙ ΤΑΕΙ Τ[Ε ΤΜΝ͞Τ]ΕΡΟ Ν͞ΜΠΗΥΕ ΚΑΛΩC
25 ΑΠΧΟΕΙC ΧΟΟ[C Χ]Ε ΑΖΟΕΙΝΕ ΒΩΚ˙ ΕΤΜΝ͞
˴Τ˴ΕΡΟ Ν͞ΜΠΗΥ[Ε] ˴Ε˴ΥCΩΒΕ ΑΥΩ ΑΥΕΙ ΕΒΟΛ
[.......] Α˴Υ˴[....] ΟΥΑ ΧΕ ΟΥΧΡΗCΤΙΑΝΟC
[.....] ˴ΕΚ˴[......]˴Ο˴Ν ΑΥΩ Ν͞ΤΕΥΝΟΥ
[ΑϤΕΙ ΕϤΒΗΚ ΕΠΙ]ΤΝ͞ ΕΠΜΟΟΥ ΑϤΕΙ
30 [ΕΠCΑ Ν͞ΤΠΕ ΕϤΧΟCΕ] ΑΠΤΗΡϤ˙ ΕΤΒΕ
[ΠΑΕΙ........ ΟΥΠ]ΑΙΓΝΙΟΝ ΠΕ ΑΛ
[ΛΑ ΑϤΡ̄ΚΑΤΑΦ]ΡΟΝΕΙ Μ͞ΠΕΕΙΠΕ
[ΛϬΕ ΕϤΟ ΜΠϢΑ Α]Ν˙ ΕΤΜΝ͞ΤΕΡΟ ΝΜ͞
[ΠΗΥΕ........] ˴Ε˴ϤϢΑϤ̄ΚΑΤΑΦΡΟΝΕΙ
35 [Μ͞ΜΟϤ.... ΑΥ]Ω Ν͞ϤϢΟCϤ˙ ΖΩC ΠΑΙΓΝΙ
[ΟΝ ϤΝΑΕΙ ΕΒ]˴Ο˴Λ˴ ΕϤCΩΒΕ ΤΕΕΙΖΕ ΟΝ ΤΕ

The Father gives unction [breath, light] to the Son;

the Son gives it to the apostles, and the apostles transmit it
to us.

Whoever is anointed participates in plenitude;

they are resurrected; and the light, the cross, and the Holy
Spirit are in them.

This is revealed to them by the Father in the bridal chamber.

96 The Father is in the Son, and the Son is in the Father.

Such is the Kingdom of Heaven.

97 Some wished to enter the kingdom of heaven

by despising the world;

they left it, and were not Christians.

[PAGE 77, PLATE 123]

ϨΙ ΠΟΕΙΚ' ΜΝ̄ ΠΠ.Ο.[Τ].Η.Ρ.Ι.ΟΝ' ΜΝ̄ ΠΝΗϨ
ΚΑΝ ΟΥΝ̄ ΚΕΟΥΑ ΕϤϪΟΣΕ ΕΝΑΕΙ ΑΠ'
ΚΟΣΜΟΣ ϢΩΠΕ ϨΝ̄ ΟΥΠΑΡΑΠΤΩΜΑ
ΠΕΝΤΑϨΤΑΜΙΟϤ ΓΑΡ' ΝΕϤ'ΟΥΩϢ' ΑΤΑ
5 ΜΙΟϤ' ΕϤΟ Ν̄ΑΤ'ΤΑΚΟ ΑΥΩ ΝΑΘΑΝΑΤΟΣ
ΑϤϨΕ ΕΒΟΛ ΑΥΩ Μ̄ΠΕϤ'ΜΕΤΕ ΑΘΕΛΠΙΣ
ΝΕΣϢΟΟΠ' ΓΑΡ ΑΝ Ν̄ϬΙ ΤΜΝ̄ΤΑΤΤΕΚΟ
Μ̄ΠΚΟΣΜΟΣ ΑΥΩ ΝΕϤϢΟΟΠ' ΑΝ Ν̄ϬΙ
ΤΜΝ̄ΤΑΤ'ΤΑΚΟ Μ̄ΠΕΝΤΑϨΤΑΜΙΕ ΠΚΟΣ
10 ΜΟΣ ΣϢΟΟΠ ΓΑΡ ΑΝ Ν̄ϬΙ ΤΜΝ̄ΤΑΤΤΑ
ΚΟ Ν̄Ν̄ϨΒΗΥΕ ΑΛΛΑ Ν̄Ν̄ϢΗΡΕ ΑΥΩ ΜΝ̄
ΟΥϨΩΒ' ΝΑϢ ϪΙ Ν̄ΟΥΜΝ̄ΤΑΤΤΑΚΟ ΕϤΤΜ
ϢΩΠΕ Ν̄ϢΗΡΕ ΠΕΤΕ ΜΝ̄ ϬΟΜ ΔΕ Μ̄ΜΟϤ'
ΕϪΙ ΠΟΣΩ ΜΑΛΛΟΝ ϤΝΑϢ ✝ ΑΝ ΠΠΟΤΗ
15 ΡΙΟΝ' Μ̄ΠϢΛΗΛ ΟΥΝ̄ΤΑϤ ΗΡΠ' Μ̄ΜΑΥ ΟΥ
Ν̄ΤΑϤ' ΜΟΟΥ ΕϤ'ΚΗ ΕϨΡΑΪ ΕΠΤΥΠΟΣ · Μ̄
ΠΕΣΝΟϤ' ΕΤΟΥΡ̄ΕΥΧΑΡΙΣΤΕΙ ΕϪΩϤ ΑΥ
Ω ϤΜΟΥϨ ΕΒΟΛ ϨΜ̄ ΠΠΝ̄Ᾱ ΕΤΟΥΑΑΒ' ΑΥ
Ω ΠΑ ΠΤΕΛΕΙΟΣ ΤΗΡϤ Ρ̄Ρ̄ΩΜΕ ΠΕ ϨΟΤᾹ

[PAGE 77, PLATE 123]

98   There are some who go into the water,

and when they emerge, they recognize the Presence in

everything.

This is why there is nothing to be despised;

a king in rags is still a king.

Those who mock him will not enter into his kingdom.

Likewise, one must not mock the bread, the chalice, and the

unity,[44]

even though they are only symbols.

99   What we call the world is not the real world; but if we could

see it with the eyes of the Being who infuses it, we would

see it as incorruptible and immortal. The fall consists in

aiming away from the object of desire.

What we call the world has always been transient;

nothing can receive incorruptibility

that is not grounded in a filial relation;

if someone does not know how to receive, how can they give?

100   The cup [*poterion*] of communion contains wine, and also

water; both are

---

44. [Previous English translations of the Gospel of Philip read "oil" here.
See www.metalog.org/ and www.gnosis.org/naghamm/nhl.html. —*Trans.*]

20 ЄNˈϢΑΝСⲰ ⲘΠΑЄΙ ΤΝΑϪΙ ΝΑΝ ⲘΠΤЄ
ΛЄΙОС Ⲣ̄ⲢⲰΜЄ ΠΜООⲨ ЄΤОΝⲌ ОⲨСⲰΜΑ
ΠЄ ϢϢЄ ЄΤⲢⲚ̄ϯ ⳍΙⲰⲰΝ ⲘΠⲢⲰΜЄ ЄΤОΝⳍ
ЄΤΒЄ ΠΑЄΙ ЄϤЄΙ ЄϤΒΗΚ ЄΠΙΤⲚ̄ ЄΠΜО
ОⲨ ϢΑϤΚΑΚϤ ΑⳍΗⲨ ϢΙΝΑ ЄϤΝΑϯ ΠΗ

25 ⳍΙⲰⲰϤ` ϢΑⲢЄОⲨⳍΤО ϪΠЄ ОⲨⳍΤО ОⲨ
ⲢⲰΜЄ ϢΑⲢЄϤ`ϪΠЄ ⲢⲰΜЄ ОⲨΝОⲨΤЄ
ϢΑⲢЄϤϪΠЄ ΝОⲨΤЄ ΤΑЄΙ ΤЄ ΘЄ ⳍ̣Μ̄. [ΠΠΑΤ]
ϢЄΛЄЄΤ` ΜⲚ̄ ⳍⲚ̄ .Τ.[ϢЄΛ].ЄЄΤ. Α.Ⲩ.[ϢⲰ]
ΠЄ ЄΒОΛ ⳍⲘ̄ ΠΝ[ⲨΜΦⲰΝ Ν̄ϬΙ ΝЄⲨϢΗⲢЄ]

30 ΝЄΜⲚ̄ ΙОⲨΔΑΙ .Ϣ.[ООΠ ОΝ ЄⲨϢⲰΠЄ]
ЄΒОΛ ⳍⲚ̄ Ν̄ⳍЄ[ΛΛΗΝ ⳍОСОΝ ЄΠΝОΜОС]
ϢООΠ` ΑⲨⲰ Α[ΝОΝ ⳍⲰⲰΝ ΑΝϢⲰΠЄ]
ЄΒОΛ ⳍⲚ̄ Ν̄ΙОⲨΔ.Α.[Ι ЄΜΠΑΤⲚ̄ϢⲰΠЄ]
Ν̄ΧⲢΙСΤΙΑΝОС ΑΚ[........... ΑⲨ]

35 Ⲱ ΑⲨΜОⲨΤЄ ΑΝЄЄΙ.ΜΑ.[........ϪЄ]
ΠⲄЄΝОС ЄΤСОΤΠ` ⲘΠ[ΠΝ̄Ᾱ ЄΤОⲨΑΑΒ]

symbols of the blood of blessing [*eukharistia*];

the cup is filled with the Holy Spirit, it is the cup of the
   realized Human Being.

If we drink from it, we enter into fullness.

101   The water of life is a body [*soma*].

We must clothe the living Human Being;

if someone is immersed in this water,

they shed their old clothes to put on the new.

102   A horse begets a horse,

a human begets a human,

a god begets a god;

the children of the union of Lover and Beloved

are born in the bridal chamber.

As long as the law remains, no Jew can be born of a Greek,

yet Christians come from Jews.

There is yet another race animated by the Breath:

These are the true human beings, the Sons of Man, the Sons
   of the Son.[45]

These true human beings are called to love in the world.

---

45. See note 39.

[PAGE 78, PLATE 124]

ΑΥШ ΠΑΛΗΘΕΙ.Ν.ΟС Ῥ.ΡШΜΕ ΑΥШ ΠϢΗΡΕ

ΜΠΡШΜΕ ΑΥШ ΠСΠΕΡΜΑ ΜΠϢΗΡΕ ΜΠΡШ

ΜΕ ΠΕΕΙΓΕΝΟС ῩΑΛΗΘΕΙΝΟΝ СΕῬΟΝΟ

ΜΑΖΕ ΜΜΟЧ˙ ΖῙ ΠΚΟСΜΟС ΝΑΕΙ ΝΕ ΠΜΑ

5 ΕΤΟΥϢΟΟΠ˙ ΜΜΑΥ ῩϬΙ ῩϢΗΡΕ ΜΠΝΥΜ

ΦШΝ ΕΠΖШΤῬ ϢΟΟΠ · ΖῙ ΠΕΕΙΚΟСΜΟС

[Ζ]ΟΟΥΤ ΖΙ СΖΙΜΕ ΠΜΑ ΕΤϬΟΜ ΜῩ ΤΜΝΤ̄

ϬШΒ ΖῙ ΠΑΙШΝ ΚΕΟΥΑ ΠΕ ΠΕΙΝΕ ΜΠΖШ

ΤῬ ΕΜ˙ΜΟΥΤΕ ΔΕ ΕΡΟΟΥ ῩΝΕΕΙΡΑΝ ΟΥΝ ΖῩ

10 ΚΟΟΥΕ ΔΕ ϢΟΟΠ˙ СΕΧΟСΕ ΠΑΡΑ ΡΑΝ˙

ΝΙΜ ΕΤΟΥῬΟΝΟΜΑΖΕ ΜΜΟΟΥ ΑΥШ С.Ε.

ΧΟΟСΕ ΕΠΧШΡΕ ΠΜΑ ΓΑΡ ΕΤΕ ΟΥῩ ΒΙΑ

ΜΜΑΥ ΕΥϢΟΟΠ˙ ΜΜΑΥ ῩϬΙ ΝΕΤ˙СΟΤΠ˙

ΕΤϬΟΜ ΝΕΤΜΜΑΥ ΚΕΟΥΑ ΑΝ ΠΕ ΑΥШ ΚΕ

15 ΟΥΑ ΠΕ ΑΛΛΑ ῩΤΟΟΥ ΜΠΕСΝΑΥ ΠΙΟΥΑ

ΟΥШΤ˙ ΠΕ ΠΑΕΙ ΠΕ ΕΤЧΝΑϢ Ι ΑΝ ΕΖΡΑΪ

ΕΧῩ ΦΗΤ ῩСΑΡΖ ΟΥΟΝ˙ ΝΙΜ ΕΤΟΥΝΤΟΥ

ΠΤΗΡЧ˙ ΜΜΑΥ ϢϢΕ ΑΝ ΕΤΡΟΥΕΙΜΕ Μ

ΜΜΟΟΥ ΤΗΡΟΥ ΖΟΕΙΝΕ ΜΕΝ ΕΥΤΜΕΙΜΕ

[PAGE 78, PLATE 124]

103–104 Wherever they are, they remain the children of the bridal
chamber.

A certain harmony is possible in this world,

where man and woman, strength and weakness, unite with each
other.

In the Temple Space [*Aeon*], the form of union is different,

although we employ the same name for it;

but there exist forms of union higher than any that can be
spoken,

stronger than the greatest forces,

with the power that is their destiny.

Those who live this are no longer separated.

They are one, beyond bodily distinction.

105 Is it not necessary for those who know

this fullness to recognize each other?

Yet some do not;

they are deprived of this joy.

Those who recognize each other

know the joy [*apolenein*] of living together in this fullness.

20 ⲘⲘⲞⲞⲨ ⲤⲈⲚⲀⲢⲀⲠⲞⲖⲀⲨⲈ ⲀⲚ ⲚⲚⲈⲦⲈ
ⲞⲨⲚⲦⲀⲨⲤⲈ ⲚⲈⲦⲀⲌⲤⲈⲂⲞ ⲆⲈ ⲈⲢⲞⲞⲨ ⲤⲈⲚⲀ
ⲢⲀⲠⲞⲖⲀⲨⲈ ⲘⲘⲞⲞⲨ ⲞⲨ ⲘⲞⲚⲞⲚ ⲠⲢⲰⲘⲈ
ⲚⲦⲈⲖⲈⲒⲞⲤ ⲤⲈⲚⲀϢ ⲈⲘⲀⳌⲦⲈ ⲀⲚ ⲘⲘⲞⳋ`
ⲀⲖⲖⲀ ⲤⲈⲚⲀϢ ⲚⲀⲨ ⲈⲢⲞⳋ ⲀⲚ ⲈⲨϢⲀⲚⲚⲀⲨ

25 ⲄⲀⲢ` ⲈⲢⲞⳋ` ⲤⲈⲚⲀⲈⲘⲀⳌⲦⲈ ⲘⲘⲞⳋ` ⲚⲔⲈⲢⲎⲦⲈ
ⲘⲚ ⲞⲨⲀ ⲚⲀϢ ϪⲠⲞ ⲚⲀⳋ` ⲚⲦⲈⲈⲒⲬⲀⲢⲒⲤ ⲈⲒ
[ⲘⲎ Ⲛ]ⳋ✝ ⸳Ⳅ⸳[Ⲓ]ⲰⲰⳋ ⲘⲠⲦⲈⲖⲈⲒⲞⲚ ⲚⲞⲨⲞⲈⲒⲚ
[ⲀⲨⲰ] Ⲛⳋ[Ϣ]Ⲱ[ⲠⲈ Ⳅ]⸳Ⲱ⸳Ⲱⳋ ⲚⲦⲈⲖⲈⲒⲞⲚ ⲞⲨⲞ
[ⲈⲒⲚ Ⲛ]⸳ⲦⲀⲢⲈⳋ⸳[✝ ⲘⲘⲞⳋ Ⳅ]ⲒⲰⲰⳋ` ⳋⲚⲀⲂⲰⲔ`

30 [ⲈⳌⲞⲨⲚ ⲠⲞⲨⲞⲈⲒⲚ] ⸳Ⲡ⸳ⲀⲈⲒ ⲠⲈ ⲠⲦⲈⲖⲈⲒⲞ̄
[ⲚⲞⲨⲞⲈⲒⲚ ⲀⲨⲰ ϢϢⲈ] ⲈⲦⲢⲚ̄ϢⲰⲠⲈ Ⲛ̄
[ⲢⲢⲰⲘⲈ Ⲛ̄ⲠⲚⲈⲨⲘⲀⲦⲒⲔ]⸳Ⲟ⸳Ⲥ ⲈⲘ`ⲠⲀⲦⲚ̄ⲈⲒ Ⲉ
[ⲂⲞⲖ ⳌⲘ̄ ⲠⲔⲞⲤⲘⲞⲤ] ⸳Ⲡ⸳ⲈⲦⲀϪⲒ ⲠⲦⲎⲢⳋ`
[ⲈⳋⲞ Ⲛ̄ϪⲞⲈⲒⲤ ⲀⲚ] ⲀⲚⲈⲈⲒⲘⲀ ⳋⲚⲀϢ Ⲣ̄

35 [ϪⲞⲈⲒⲤ ⲀⲚ ⲀⲠ]ⲘⲀ ⲈⲦⲘ̄ⲘⲀⲨ ⲀⲖⲖⲀ ⳋⲚⲀ
[ⲂⲰⲔ ⲀⲦⲘⲈⳋ]ⲞⲦⲎⲤ ⳌⲰⲤ ⲀⲦϪⲰⲔ` ⲈⲂⲞⲖ

106   Realization makes a Human Being [*Anthropos*] impalpable and
         invisible.

         If they were visible, people would enclose them within the
         bounds of the visible.

         To know the grace of true communion with Him,

         one must be clothed in clear light.

         In this light we can see His light.

107   Before leaving this world, we must become human beings
         inhabited by the Breath.

         Whoever receives fullness without truly welcoming it

         is not yet in Peace.

         They will wander in the intermediate world of their
         incompletion.

[PAGE 79, PLATE 125]

ΜΟΝΟΝ ΙC̄ CΟΟΥ.Ν, Μ̄ΠΤΕΛΟC Μ̄ΠΑΕΙ
ΠΡⲰΜΕ ΕΤΟΥΑΑΒ ΨΟΥΑΑΒ ΤΗΡϤ‵ ϢΑ Ƨ
ΡΑΪ ΕΠΕϤ‵CⲰΜΑ ΕϢΧΕ ΑϤΧΙ ΓΑΡ Μ̄ΠΟ
ΕΙΚ‵ ϤΝΑΑϤ‵ ΕϤ‵ΟΥΑΑΒ Η ΠΠΟΤΗΡΙΟΝ .
5 Η ΠΚΕCΕΕΠΕ ΤΗΡϤ‵ ΕΤϤΧΙ Μ̄ΜΟΟΥ ΕϤ‵
ΤΟΥΒΟ Μ̄ΜΟΟΥ ΑΥⲰ ΠⲰC ϤΝΑΤΟΥΒΟ
ΑΝ Μ̄ΠΚΕCⲰΜΑ Ν̄ΘΕ ΝΤΑΙC̄ ΧⲰΚ‵ ΕΒΟΛ
Μ̄ΠΜΟΟΥ Μ̄ΠΒΑΠΤΙCΜΑ ΤΑΕΙ ΤΕ ΘΕ ΑϤ
ΠⲰƧΤ‵ ΕΒΟΛ‵ Μ̄ΠΜΟΥ ΕΤΒΕ ΠΑΕΙ ΤΝ̄ΒΗΚ
10 ΜΕΝ ΕΠΙΤΝ̄ ΕΠΜΟΟΥ ΤΝ̄ΒΗΚ ΔΕ ΑΝ
ΕΠΙΤΝ̄ ΕΠΜΟΥ ϢΙΝΑ ΧΕ ΝΟΥΠΑƧΤΝ̄
ΕΒΟΛ ƧΜ̄ ΠΠΝ̄Ᾱ Μ̄ΠΚΟCΜΟC ƧΟΤΑΝ
ΕϤϢΑΝΝΙϤΕ ϢΑΡΕϤ‵ΤΕΤΠΡⲰ ϢⲰΠΕ
ΠΠΝ̄Ᾱ ΕΤΟΥΑΑΒ ƧΟΤΑΝ ΕϤ‵ϢΑΝΝΙϤΕ
15 ϢΑΡΕΤϢΑΜΗ ϢⲰΠΕ ΠΕΤΕΥΝ̄ΤΑϤ ‵Μ̄
ΜΑΥ Ν̄ΤΓΝⲰCΙC Ν̄ΤΜΕ ΟΥΕΛΕΥΘΕΡΟC
ΠΕ ΠΕΛΕΥΘΕΡΟC ΔΕ ΜΑϤϤ Ρ̄ ΝΟΒΕ ΠΕ
ϯΡΕ ΓΑΡ Μ̄ΠΝΟΒΕ ΠƧΜ̄Ƨ̄ᾹΛ Μ̄ΠΝΟΒΕ
ΠΕ ΤΜΑΑΥ ΤΕ ΤΑΛΗΘΕΙΑ ΤΓΝⲰCΙC ΔΕ

[PAGE 79, PLATE 125]

Only Yeshua knows the end of all that is becoming.

108 The holiness of the Saints includes their body [*soma*].

They bless the bread and break it,

and all that they touch is purified.

How could their body not also be purified?

109 Yeshua blessed the waters of baptism,

and rid them of their power of dissolution;

this is why we can be submerged in them without dying,

and in them receive a breath different from that of the world.

When the latter breathes in us, it gives rise to winter;

when the Holy Spirit breathes in us, it gives rise to spring.

110 Whoever has knowledge [*gnosis*] of the truth is free [*eleutheros*]; the free human being is righteous.

Those who transgress are the slaves of transgression.[46]

---

46. Cf. John 8:34.

20 ΠΕ ΠΤΩΤ' ΝΕΤΕ CTO NAY AN AР̄ NOBE
ЄΠΚΟCΜΟC ΜΟΥΤΕ ЄΡΟΟΥ ЖЄ ЄΛЄΥ
ΘΕΡΟC ΝΑΕΙ ЄΤCTO NAY AN AР̄ NOBE
ΤΓΝΩCIC Ν̄ΤΑΛΗΘΕΙΑ ЖICЄ Ν̄ϨΗΤ' ЄΤЄ
ΠΑΕΙ ΠΕ CЄΙΡЄ Μ̄ΜΟΟΥ Ν̄ЄΛЄΥΘΕΡΟC
25 ΑΥΩ CΤΡΟΥЖICЄ ЄΠΜΑ ΤΗΡϤ' ΤΑΓΑΠΗ
ΔΕ ΚΩΤ' ΠΕΤΑϨР̄ ЄΛЄΥΘΕΡΟC ΔΕ ϨΙ
ΤΝ̄ ΤΓΝΩCIC ϤΟ Ν̄ϨΜϨ̄ᾹΛ̄ ЄΤΒΕ ΤΑΓΑ
ΠΗ Ν̄ΝΑΕΙ ЄΜΠΑΤΟΥϢ ϤΙ ЄϨΡΑ[Ϊ ΝΤЄ]
ΛЄΥΘΕΡΙΑ Ν̄Τ.Γ.ΝΩCIC .Τ.ΓΝΩ[CIC ΔЄ]
30 CЄΙΡЄ Μ̄ΜΟΟΥ Ν̄ϢΙΚΑΝΟC Є.C.[ΤΡΟΥ]
ϢΩΠЄ Ν̄ЄΛ[ЄΥΘ]Є[ΡΟC Τ].Α.ΓΑΠΗ [ΜΑCЖΙ]
ΛΑΑΥ ΠЄ ΠΩ[C CΝΑЖΙ ΟΥ].ΟΝ. [ΟΥΟΝ ΝΙΜ]
ΠΩC ΠЄ ΜΑC.Ж.[ΟΟC ЖЄ ΠΑΕΙ ΠΩΕΙ ΠЄ]
Η ΠΑΕΙ ΠΩΕΙ ΠЄ [ΑΛΛΑ CЖΩ ΜΜΟC ЖЄ ΝΑΕΙ]
35 ΝΟΥΚ' ΝЄ ΤΑΓΑΠΗ Μ̄.ΠΝЄΥΜ.[ΑΤΙΚΗ]
ΟΥΗΡΠ' ΤЄ ϨΙ CΤΟΕΙ CЄР̄ΑΠ.Ο.[ΛΑΥЄ Μ̄]

Truth is our mother; knowledge [*gnosis*] is the promise of our
  union with her.

Those who do not go astray are called free by the world;

the knowledge of truth lifts their heart,

making them free of all bonds;

it is love which makes them act.

Those who have become free through knowledge

become loving servants of those who do not yet have this
  knowledge and freedom.

Knowledge [*gnosis*] makes them capable of this

because they are free, even of their freedom.

Love refuses nothing, and takes nothing;

it is the highest and vastest freedom.

All exists through love.

It does not say "this is mine," but "this is yours."

111   Spiritual Love [*agapē pneumatikos*] is a drunkenness and a
  balm;

those who are anointed by it rejoice.

[PAGE 80, PLATE 126]

ΜΟС ΤΗΡΟΥ Ν̄.Ꚇ̣[Ι Ν]ΕΤΝΑΤΟϨϹΟΥ Μ̄ΜΟϹ
ϹΕΡ̄ΑΠΟΛΑΥΕ ϨΩΟΥ Ñ̄ϬΙ ΝΕΤΑϨΕΡΑΤΟΥ
Μ̄ΠΟΥΒΟΛ ϨΩϹ ΕΥΑϨΕΡΑΤΟΥ Ñ̄ϬΙ ΝΕΤˋ
ΤΟϨϹ ΝΕΤΤΑϨϚ̄ Ñ̄ϹΟϬΝ ΕΥϢΑΛΟ ΕΤΟΥ
5 ΩΟΥ Ñ̄ϹΕΒΩΚˋ ϢΑΡΕΝΗ ΕϹΕΤΟϨϹ ΑΝ
ΜΟΝΟΝ ΕΥΑϨΕ ΕΡΑΤΟΥ Μ̄ΠΟΥΒΑΛ ϢΑΥ
ϬΩ ΟΝ ϨΜ̄ ΠΟΥϹ†ΒΩΩΝ ΠϹΑΜΑΡΙΤΗϹ
Ñ̄ΤΑϤˋ† ΛΑΑΥ ΑΝˋ ΑΠΕΤϢΟΟϬΕ ΕΙΜΗ
ΗΡΠˋ ϨΙ ΝΕϨ ΚΕΛΑΑΥ ΑΝ ΠΕ ΕΙΜΗΤΙˋ Α
10 ΠϹΟϬΝ ΑΥΩ ΑϤΘΕΡΑΠΕΥΕ Ν̄Μ̄ΠΛΗΓΗ
ΤΑΓΑΠΗ ΓΑΡ ϨΩΒϚ̄ Ñ̄ΟΥΜΗΗϢΕ Ñ̄ΝΟ
ΒΕ ΠΕΤΕ ΤϹϨΙΜΕ ΜΕ Μ̄ΜΟϤˋ ΝΕΤˋϹΝΑ
ΧΠΟΟΥ ΕΥΕΙΝΕ Μ̄ΜΟϤˋ ΕϢΩΠΕ ΠΕϹ
ϨΑΕΙ ΕΥΕΙΝΕ Μ̄ΠΕϹϨΑΙ ΕϢΩΠΕ ΟΥΝΟ
15 ΕΙΚˋ ΠΕ ΕΥΕΙΝΕ Μ̄ΠΝΟΕΙΚˋ ΠΟΛΛΑΚΙϹ
ΕϢΩΠΕ ΟΥÑ̄ ϹϨΙΜΕ ΕϹÑ̄ΚΟΤΚˋ ΜÑ̄ ΠΕϹ
ϨΑΪ ΚΑΤΑ ΟΥϨΤΟΡˋ ΕΠΕϹϨΤ ΔΕ ϨΙ ΠΝΟ
ΕΙΚ ΕϢΑϹΡ̄ΚΟΙΝΩΝΕΙ ΝΜ̄ΜΑϤˋ ΠΕΤˋ
ϹΑΜΑϹΤϤˋ ϢΑϹΜΑϹΤϤˋ ΕϤΙΝΕ Μ̄ΠΝΟ

[PAGE 80, PLATE 126]

Those who do not belong to the community may also rejoice
in it,

for they benefit from its proximity;

but if they depart from it, they lose its perfume and its unction,

and are left with their natural odors.

The Samaritan gives only wine and oil to the wounded.

Unction heals all wounds,

for love heals us of the multitude of our wanderings.[47]

112   A woman's children resemble the man she loves.

When it is her husband, they resemble the husband.

When it is her lover, they resemble the lover.

Often, when a woman unites with her husband out of
obligation,

yet her heart is with a lover with whom she is frequently
uniting,

her offspring will resemble her lover.

---

47. Cf. 1 Peter 4:8.

20 ЄІК' ҢТѠТҢ ΔЄ ΝЄТѰΟΟΠ' ΜΝ ΠѰΗ

РЄ ΜΠΝΟΥΤЄ ΜΝΜΡ̄ΡЄ ΠΚΟСΜΟС`

ΑλλΑ ΜΡ̄ΡЄ ΠΧΟЄІС ѰІΝΑ ΝЄΤЄΤΝΑ

ΧΠΟΟΥ ΝΟΥѰѠΠЄ ЄΥЄІΝЄ ΜΠΚΟС

ΜΟС ΑλλΑ ЄΥΝΑѰѠΠЄ ЄΥЄІΝЄ ΜΠ

25 ΧΟЄІС ѰΑΡЄΠΡѠΜЄ ΤѠ2 ΜΝ ΠΡѠΜЄ

ѰΑΡЄΠ2ΤΟ ΤѠ2 ΜΝ Π2ΤΟ ѰΑΡЄΠЄІ

[Ѡ Т].Ѡ.2 ΜΝ ΠЄІѠ ҢΓЄΝΟС ΝЄѰΑΥΤѠ2

[ΜΝ] .Ν.ΟΥѰ.Β.Ρ̄ ΓЄΝΟС ΤΑЄІ ΤЄ ΘЄ ЄѰΑ

[РЄΠ]ΠΝ̄Ā ΤѠ2 ΜΝ ΠΠΝ̄Ā ΑΥѠ ΠλΟ

30 [ΓΟС] .Ѱ.ΑϤΡ̄Κ[ΟІ].Ν.[ѠΝ]ЄІ ΜΝ ΠλΟΓΟС

[ΑΥѠ ΠΟ]Υ.Ο.[ЄІΝ ѰΑϤ]Ρ̄ΚΟІΝѠΝЄІ

[ΜΝ ΠΟΥΟЄІΝ ЄΚѰ]ΑѰѠΠЄ Ρ̄ΡѠΜЄ

[ΠΡѠΜЄ ΠЄΤΝΑΜ]ЄΡІΤΚ' ЄΚѰΑѰѠΠЄ

[ΜΠΠΝ̄Ā] ΠΠΝ̄Ā ΠЄΤΝΑ2ѠΤΡ̄ ЄΡΟΚ' ЄΚ

35 [ѰΑѰ]ѠΠЄ ҢλΟΓΟС ΠλΟΓΟС ΠЄΤ'

You who are with the Son of God do not love worldly things;

love the Teacher, so that what you engender

will resemble the Teacher, and not some other thing.

113   Humans mate with humans,

horses with horses, donkeys with donkeys,

each species with its own.

Likewise, our breath seeks another breath,

our intelligence seeks intelligence,

and every clarity seeks its light.

Become more human, and humans will love you;

become more spiritual, and the Spirit will unite with you.

Become more intelligent, and the *Logos* will unite with you.

[PAGE 81, PLATE 127]

ΝΑΤѠ2 ΝΜ̄ΜΑΚ' Ε[Κ]ΨΑΝΨѠΠΕ Ν̄ΟΥ
ΟΕΙΝ ΠΟΥΟΕΙΝ ΠΕΤΝᾹΡ̄ΚΟΙΝѠΝΕΙ
ΝΜ̄ΜΑΚ' ΕΚ'ΨΑΝΨѠΠΕ Ν̄ΝΑ ΠϹΑ Ν
2ΡΕ ΝΑ ΠϹΑ Ν2ΡΕ ΝΑΜ̄ΤΟΝ' Μ̄ΜΟΟΥ·
5   Ε2ΡΑΪ ΕΧѠΚ' ΕΚΨΑΝΨѠΠΕ Ν̄ϹΤΟ
Η Ν̄ΕΙѠ Η Μ̄ΜΑϹΕ Η Ν̄ΟΥ2ΟΟΡ' Η ΝΕ
ϹΟΟΥ Η 6Ε 2Ν̄ ΝΕΘΗΡΙΟΝ ΕΤΝ̄ΠϹΑ Ν
ΒΟΛ ΜΝ̄ ΝΕΤΜ̄ΠϹΑ ΜΠΙΤΝ̄ ΨΝΑΨ ΜΕ
ΡΙΤΚ' ΑΝ ΟΥΤΕ ΠΡѠΜΕ ΟΥΤΕ ΠΠΝ̄Α ΟΥ
10 ΤΕ ΠΛΟΓΟϹ ΟΥΤΕ ΠΟΥΟΕΙΝ ΟΥΤΕ ΝΑ
ΠϹΑ ΝΤΠΕ ΟΥΤΕ ΝΑ ΠϹΑ Ν2ΟΥΝ ϹΕ
ΝΑΨ Μ̄ΤΟΝ' Μ̄ΜΟΟΥ ΑΝ 2ΡΑΪ Ν̄2ΗΤΚ'
ΑΥѠ ΜΝ̄ΤΑΚ' ΜΕΡΟϹ 2ΡΑΪ Ν̄2ΗΤΟΥ ΠΕ
ΤΟ Ν̄2Μ̄2̄ᾹΛ̄ Ε2ΝΑΨ' ΑΝ ΨΝΑΨ Ρ̄ ΕΛΕΥ
15 ΘΕΡΟϹ ΠΕΝΤΑ2Ρ̄ ΕΛΕΥΘΕΡΟϹ Μ̄ΠΕ2
ΜΟΤ' Μ̄ΠΕΨΧΟΕΙϹ ΑΥѠ ΑΨΤΑΑΨ' ΕΒΟΛ
ΟΥΑΑΨ' ΑΥΜΝ̄Τ̄2Μ̄2̄ᾹΛ̄ ΟΥΚΕΤΙ ΨΝΑΨ
Ρ̄ ΕΛΕΥΘΕΡΟϹ ΤΜ̄ΝΤΟΥΟΕΙΕ Μ̄ΠΚΟϹ
ΜΟϹ 2ΙΤΝ̄ ΨΤΟΟΥ Ν̄ΕΙΔΟϹ ΨΑΥΟΛΟΥ

[PAGE 81, PLATE 127]

If you become more clear, the light will unite with you.

If you ascend, you will find repose in the heights.

If you behave like a horse or donkey, calf, dog, sheep, or any
other animal outside yourself,

you will be capable of union with neither human, spirit,
Logos, nor light,

nor with what is above, nor with what is within.

None of these realities can settle in you if you do not become
like them through love.

114　Whoever is a slave against their will has the possibility of
becoming free.

But the one who has become free by the grace of the Teacher,

and who has chosen to be a slave,

how could they then choose to be free again?

20 ЄϨΟΥΝ ΑΤΑΠΟΘΗΚΗ ϨΙΤÑ ΟΥΜΟΟΥ
ΜÑΝ ΟΥΚΑϨ ΜÑΝ ΟΥΠÑᾹ ΜÑΝ ΟΥΟΕΙ[Ν]
ΑΥⲰ ΤΜÑΤΟΥΕΙΕ ̄ΜΠΝΟΥΤΕ ΤΕΕΙϨΕ
ΟΝ ϨΙΤÑ ϤΤΟΟΥ ϨΙΤÑ ΟΥΠΙСΤΙС ΜÑ
Ν ΟΥϨΕΛΠΙС ΜÑΝ ΟΥΑΓΑΠΗ ΜÑ ΟΥ

25 ΓΝⲰСΙС ΠÑΚΑϨ ΤΕ Τ'ΠΙСΤΙС ΤΑΪ ΕΝ'
ϪΕ ΝΟΥΝΕ ϨΡΑΪ Ñ2ΗΤ͞С ΠΜΟ[ΟΥ]
ΤΕ ΘΕΛΠΙС ΕΒΟΛ ϨΙΤΟΟΤ͞С Ε[ΝСΟ]
ΕΙϢ ΠΠÑᾹ ΤΕ ΤΑΓΑΠΗ ΕΒΟΛ [ϨΙΤΟ]
ΟΤϤ' ΕΝΑΥϪΑ.Ν.Ε ΠΟΥΟΕΙΝ Δ[Ε ΤΕ]

30 ΤΓΝⲰСΙС ΕΒ[ΟΛ ϨΙΤΟΟ]Τ͞С .ΤÑΠ.[Ⲱ2]
ΤϪΑΡΙС СΟ Ñ.Ϥ.[Ο ΑΥⲰ ΤΝΑΠΡΕ ̄ΜΠ]
ΡΜÑΚΑϨ СΟ Ρ̄Ρ[ⲰΜΕ ΕΤΟΥΒΗΚ ΑΠСΑ Ñ]
ΤΠΕ ÑΤΕ ΤΠΕ ΑΥ[Ⲱ Π]Ϩ.Μ.[ϨΑΛ ΜΑΚΑ]
ΡΙΟС ΠΕ ΠΑΕΙ ΕΜ'ΠΕϤΛ.Λ.[ΥΠΕΙ Ñ]

115 What is harvested in the world is composed of four elements:

water, earth, wind, and light.

What God harvests is also composed of

four elements: faith [*pistis*], hope [*elpis*], love [*agapē*], and

contemplation [*gnosis*].

Our earth is faith, for she gives us roots.

Water is our hope, for it slakes our thirst.

Wind [*pneuma*] is the love [*agapē*] through which we grow;

and light is the contemplation [*gnosis*] through which we ripen.

116 Grace is transmitted to us in four ways:

the work of the earth, the taste of the heavens,

and love and truth, which are beyond the heavens.

Blessed is the one who makes no sadness in the soul.

That one is Jesus Christ.

[PAGE 82, PLATE 128]

ΝΟΥΨΥΧΗ ΠΑΕΙ ΠΕ Ι̅C̅ ΠΧ̅C̅ ΑϤⲢΑΠΑ̅

ΤΑ Μ̅ΠΜΑ ΤΗΡϤˋ ΑΥΩ Μ̅ΠΕϤⲢⲂΑΡΕΙ Λ̅ΛΑΑΥ

ΕΤΒΕ ΠΑΕΙ · ΟΥΜΑΚΑΡΙΟC ΠΕ ΠΑΕΙ Ν̅ΤΕΕΙ

ΜΙΝΕ ΧΕ ΟΥΤΕΛΕΙΟC Ρ̅ΡΩΜΕ ΠΕ ΠΑΕΙ ΓΑΡ

5 ΠΛΟΓΟC ΧΝΟΥΝˋ Μ̅ΜΟΝ ΕΡΟϤˋ ΖΩCΜΟΚΖ

ΑCΕΖΕ ΠΑΕΙ ΕΡΑΤϤˋ ΠΩC ΤΝ̅ΝΑϢ Ρ̅ΚΑΤΟΡ

ΘΟΥ Μ̅ΠΕΕΙΝΟ6 ΠΩC ΕϤΝΑ† ΑΝΑΠΑΥ

CΙC Ν̅ΟΥΟΝˋ ΝΙΜ ΖΑ ΤΕ2Η Ν̅2ΩΒ ΝΙΜ ϢϢΕ

ΑΝ ΕΛ̅ΛΥΠΕΙ Λ̅ΛΑΑΥ ΕΙΤΕ ΝΟ6 ΕΙΤΕ ΚΟΥΕΙ

10 Η ΑΠΙCΤΟC Η ΠΙCΤΟC ΕΙΤΑ Α† ΑΝΑΠΑΥCΙC

Ν̅ΝΕΤΜ̅ΤΟΝ Μ̅ΜΟΟΥ 2Ν̅ ΝΕΤΝΑΝΟΥΟΥ

ΟΥΝ̅ 2ΟΕΙΝΕ ΕΤΟΥΝΟϤΡΕ ΤΕ Ε† ΑΝΑ

ΠΑΥCΙC Μ̅ΠΕΤϢΟΟΠˋ ΚΑΛΩC ΠΕ†ΡΕ

Μ̅ΠΕΤΝΑΝΟΥϤˋ ΜΝ̅ 6ΟΜˋ Μ̅ΜΟϤ Ν̅Ϥ†

15 ΑΝΑΠΑΥCΙC Ν̅ΝΑΕΙ ϤΙ ΓΑΡ ΑΝˋ Μ̅ΠΕΤΕ 2

ΝΑϤˋ ΜΝ̅ 6ΟΜ ΔΕ Μ̅ΜΟϤ ΑΛΛΥΠΕΙˋ ΕϤˋ

ΤΜ̅ΤΡΟΥΡ̅ΘΛΙΒΕ Μ̅ΜΟΟΥ ΑΛΛΑ ΠΕΤϢΩ

ΠΕ ΚΑΛΩC 2Ν̅CΟΠˋ ϢΑϤˋΛ̅ΛΥΠΕΙ Μ̅ΜΟ

ΟΥ ϤϢΟΟΠˋ ΑΝ Ν̅ΤΕΕΙ2Ε ΑΛΛΑ ΤΟΥΚΑ

[PAGE 82, PLATE 128]

He comes to all places, and burdens no one.

Blessed are they who act in this way;

they are realized human beings,

and the *Logos* abides in them.

117   Tell us how to rectify ourselves,

how to accomplish such a great thing,

and know repose?

118   Above all, it is befitting not to make anyone sad [*lupein*],

whether they are great, small, faithful, or unfaithful . . . then,

to bring peace to those who take pleasure in goodness.

One might think to find pleasure

in bringing peace to those who do good,

but that happens beyond the play of wills.

20 ΚΙΑ ΤΕ ΕΤΡ̄ΛΥΠΕΙ ⲘⲘΟΟΥ ΠΕΤΕΥⲚ̄ΤΑϤ'
ⲘΜΑΥ Ⲛ̄ΤϤΥСΙС ϤΤ ΟΥΝΟϤ Μ̄ΠΕΤΝΑ
ΝΟΥϤ' ϨΟΕΙΝΕ ΔΕ ΕΒΟΛ ϨⲚ̄ ΠΑΕΙ ΕΕⲖ
.Λ.ΥΠΕΙ ΚΑΚⲰС ΟΥϪΕС ϨⲚ̄ΝΗΕΙ' ΑϤϪΠΕ
Ⲛ̄ΚΑ ΝΙΜ ΕΙΤΕ ϢΗΡΕ ΕΙΤΕ ϨΜϨ̄ⲀⲖ ΕΙΤΕ
25 .ΤΒΝ.Η ΕΙΤΕ ΟΥϨΟΡ ΕΙΤΕ ΡΙΡ ΕΙΤΕ СΟΥΟ
[ΕΙΤΕ Ε]ΙⲰΤ' ΕΙΤΕ ΤⲰϨ ΕΙΤΕ ΧΟΡΤΟС ΕΙΤΕ
[ΚΕΕС] ΕΙΤΕ ΑϤ ΑΥⲰ ΒΑΛΑΝΟС ΟΥСΑΒΕ
[ΔΕ Π]Ε ΑΥⲰ ΑϤΕΙΜΕ Ⲛ̄Τ'ΤΡΟΦΗ Μ̄ΠΟΥΑ
[ΠΟΥΑ] Ⲛ̄.Ϣ.Η.Ρ.[Ε Μ].ΕΝ. [Α]ϤΚΕ ΑΡΤΟС ϨΑΡⲰ
30 [ΟΥ Ϩ1 ΝΕϨ Ϩ1 ΑϤ Ⲛ̄Ϩ]ΜϨ̄ⲀⲖ ΔΕ ΑϤΚΕ ΚΙ
[ΚΙ ϨΑΡⲰΟΥ Ϩ1 Ε]ΒΡΕ ΑΥⲰ Ⲛ̄ΤΒΝΟΟΥ
[ΑϤΝΕϪ ΕΙ].Ⲱ.[Τ ϨΑ]ΡⲰΟΥ Ϩ1 ΤⲰϨ Ϩ1 ΧΟΡ
[ΤΟС Ⲛ̄ΟΥ]ϨΟΟΡ' ΑϤΝΕϪ ΚΕΕС ϨΑΡⲰΟΥ'
[Ⲛ̄ΡΙΡ ΔΕ ΑϤ]ΝΕϪ ΒΑΛΑΝΟС ϨΑΡⲰΟΥ

The happy man or woman cannot oppress or cause misery;

yet sometimes others may be jealous of their peace and

happiness.

This causes suffering, but it is not their doing;

their nature [*phusis*] is only to give joy.

119   A great landowner had sons, servants, livestock, dogs, pigs,

wheat, barley, hay, grass, bones, meat, and acorns.

In his wisdom he gave to each what was appropriate.

To his children, he gave bread, olive oil, and meat;

to his servants, he gave oil and wheat;

to his livestock he gave barley, hay, and grass;

and he threw bones to the dogs and acorns and bread crumbs to

the pigs.

[PAGE 83, PLATE 129]

ⲌⲒ ⲘⲀⲘⲞⲨ ⲚⲞⲈⲒⲔ' ⲦⲀⲈⲒ ⲦⲈ ⲐⲈ ⲘⲠⲘⲀⲐⲎ
ⲦⲎⲤ ⲘⲠⲚⲞⲨⲦⲈ ⲈⲰⲰⲠⲈ ⲞⲨⲤⲀⲂⲈ ⲠⲈ ⲈⲤ
ⲀⲒⲤⲐⲀⲚⲈ ⲚⲦⲘⲚⲦⲘⲀⲐⲎⲦⲎⲤ ⲘⲘⲞⲢ'
ⲪⲎ ⲚⲤⲰⲘⲀⲦⲒⲔⲎ ⲤⲈⲚⲀⲢⲀⲠⲀⲦⲀ ⲀⲚ' Ⲙ
5 ⲘⲞⲨ ⲀⲖⲖⲀ' ⲈⲤⲚⲀϬⲰⲰⲦ ⲚⲤⲀ ⲦⲆⲒⲀⲐⲈ
ⲤⲒⲤ ⲚⲦⲈⲨ'ⲮⲨⲬⲎ ⲘⲠⲞⲨⲀ ⲠⲞⲨⲀ ⲚⲨⲰⲀ
ϪⲈ ⲚⲘⲘⲀϤ' ⲞⲨⲚ ⲌⲀⲌ ⲚⲐⲎⲢⲒⲞⲚ ⲌⲘ ⲠⲔⲞⲤ
ⲘⲞⲤ ⲈⲨⲞ ⲘⲘⲞⲢⲪⲎ ⲢⲢⲰⲘⲈ ⲚⲀⲈⲒ ⲈⲨ'
ⲰⲀⲤⲞⲨⲰⲚⲞⲨ ⲢⲢⲒⲢ ⲘⲈⲚ' ⲨⲚⲀⲚⲈϪ ⲂⲀ
10 ⲖⲀⲚⲞⲤ ⲈⲢⲞⲞⲨ ⲚⲦⲂⲚⲞⲞⲨ ⲆⲈ ⲨⲚⲀⲚⲈϪ
ⲈⲒⲰⲦ ⲈⲢⲞⲞⲨ ⲌⲒ ⲦⲰⲤ ⲌⲒ ⲬⲞⲢⲦⲞⲤ ⲚⲞⲨ
ⲌⲞⲞⲢ' ⲨⲚⲀⲚⲈϪ ⲔⲀⲀⲤ ⲈⲢⲞⲞⲨ ⲚⲌⲘⲌⲀⲖ
ⲨⲚⲀϮ ⲚⲀⲨ ⲚⲨⲞⲢⲠ' ⲚⲨⲎⲢⲈ ⲨⲚⲀϮ ⲚⲀⲨ
ⲚⲦⲈⲖⲈⲒⲞⲚ ⲨⲰⲞⲞⲠ' ⲚϬⲒ ⲠⲨⲎⲢⲈ ⲘⲠⲢⲰ
15 ⲘⲈ ⲀⲨⲰ ⲨⲰⲞⲞⲠ ⲚϬⲒ ⲠⲨⲎⲢⲈ ⲘⲠⲨⲎ
ⲢⲈ ⲘⲠⲢⲰⲘⲈ ⲠϪⲞⲈⲒⲤ ⲠⲈ ⲠⲨⲎⲢⲈ' Ⲙ
ⲠⲢⲰⲘⲈ ⲀⲨⲰ ⲠⲨⲎⲢⲈ ⲘⲠⲨⲎⲢⲈ' Ⲙ
ⲠⲢⲰⲘⲈ ⲠⲈ ⲠⲈⲦ'ⲤⲰⲚⲦ' ⲌⲒⲦⲘ ⲠⲨⲎ
ⲢⲈ ⲘⲠⲢⲰⲘⲈ ⲀⲠⲨⲎⲢⲈ ⲘⲠⲢⲰⲘⲈ ϪⲒ

[PAGE 83, PLATE 129]

So it is with the disciples of God.

When they are wise, they perceive the state of each.

They are not misled by outward appearances;

they consider the disposition of each soul and attune their
words accordingly.

There are many animals in the world who appear in human
form;

the wise one gives acorns to pigs, barley, hay, and grass to
livestock, bones to dogs,

to servants he gives basic lessons;

and to his children, the teaching in its entirety.

120   There are Sons of Man, and sons of Sons of Man.

The Teacher is the Son of Man,

and the grandson of Man is begotten by him.

It was from God that the Son of Man received the power to
beget.

20 ⲚⲦⲞⲞⲦϤ' ⲘⲡⲚⲞⲨⲦⲈ ⲈⲦⲢⲈϤⲤⲰⲚⲦ' ⲞⲨ
ⲦⲀϤ' ⲘⲘⲀⲨ ⲈⲦⲢⲈϤϪⲠⲞ ⲠⲈⲚⲦⲀⲋϪ Ⲓ Ⲉ
ⲦⲢⲈϤ'ⲤⲰⲚⲦ' ⲞⲨⲤⲰⲚⲦ' ⲠⲈ ⲠⲈⲚⲦⲀⲋϪⲒ
ⲈϪⲠⲞ ⲞⲨϪⲠⲞ ⲠⲈ ⲠⲈⲦⲤⲰⲚⲦ ⲘⲚ ϬⲞ[Ⲙ]
ⲚϤϪⲠⲞ ⲠⲈⲦ'ϪⲠⲞ ⲞⲨⲚ ϬⲞⲘ ⲚϤⲤⲰⲚ[Ⲧ]

25 ⲤⲈϪⲰ ⲆⲈ ⲘⲘⲞⲤ ϪⲈ ⲠⲈⲦ'ⲤⲰⲚⲦ' ϪⲠⲞ
ⲀⲖⲖⲀ ⲠⲈϤ'ϪⲠⲞ ⲞⲨⲤⲰⲚⲦ ⲠⲈ ⲈⲦ[ⲂⲈ ⲠⲀⲈⲒ]
ⲚϪⲠⲞ ⲚⲈϤ'Ⲏ̅ⲢⲈ ⲀⲚ ⲚⲈ ⲀⲖⲖⲀ .Ⲛ.[ⲈϤⳞⲒⲔⲰⲚ]
ⲚⲈ ⲠⲈⲦⲤⲰⲚⲦ' ⲈϤⲢ̅ ⲋⲰⲂ ⲋⲚ Ⲟ[ⲨⲰⲚⳞ]
ⲈⲂⲞⲖ ⲀⲨⲰ ⲚⲦⲞϤ ⲋⲰⲰϤ ϤⲞⲨ[ⲞⲚⳞ Ⲉ]

30 ⲂⲞⲖ' ⲠⲈⲦϪⲠⲞ .Ⲉ.Ϥ[Ⲣ̅ ⲋⲰⲂ] ⲋ.Ⲛ̅. [Ⲟ]Ⲩ[ⲠⲈⲐⲎⲠ]
ⲀⲨⲰ ⲚⲦⲞϤ ϤⳞ.ⲎⲠ. .Ⲡ.[ϪⲠⲞ Ⲡ]Ⲉ Ⲁ[Ⲛ ⲚⲐⲈ Ⲛ̅]
ⲐⲒⲔⲰⲚ ⲠⲈⲦ'Ⲥ.Ⲱ.[ⲚⲦ ⲘⲈⲚ] ⲈϤ.Ⲥ.[ⲰⲚⲦ ⲋⲚ]
ⲞⲨⲪⲀⲚⲈⲢⲞⲚ ⲠⲈⲦϪⲠⲞ Ⲇ[Ⲉ ⲈϤϪⲠⲞ Ⲛ̅Ⲛ]
Ⲏ̅ⲢⲈ ⲋⲚ ⲞⲨⲠⲈⲐⲎⲠ' Ⲙ.Ⲛ̅. [ⲖⲀⲀⲨ ⲚⲀⲮ]

35 ⲤⲞⲞⲨⲚ ϪⲈ ⲀⲮ ⲠⲈ Ⲫ.Ⲟ.[ⲞⲨ ⲈⲮⲀⲢⲈⲠⳞⲞⲞⲨⲦ]

121 He who has received the power to create is a creature; he who

  has received the power to beget is the son;

 he who creates cannot beget;

 but he who begets can create.

 Yet people say: "He who creates, begets";

 but what he begets is only a creature.

 They are not his children, but have his resemblance.

 He who creates works in visibility, and is himself visible.

 He who begets works in secret;

 he is hidden, and beyond all resemblance.

 He who creates, creates visibly;

 he who begets, begets his children in secret.

122 None can know the day when man and woman unite

 but themselves.

[PAGE 84, PLATE 130]

ΜΝ ΤΣϨΙΜΕ ΡΚΟΙΝΩΝΕΙ ΜΝ ΝΟΥΕΡΗΥ
ΕΙΜΗ ΝΤΟΟΥ ΟΥΑΑΥ ΟΥΜΥⲤΤΗΡΙΟΝ ΓΑΡ`
ΠΕ ΠΓΑΜΟⲤ ΜΠΚΟⲤΜΟⲤ ΝΝΕΝΤΑϨⲬΙ
ϨΙΜΕ ΕϢⲬΕ ΠΓΑΜΟⲤ ΜΠⲬΩϨΜ` ϤϨΗΠ`
5   ΠΟⲤΩ ΜΑΛΛΟΝ ΠΓΑΜΟⲤ ΝΑΤⲬΩϨΜ` ΟΥ
ΜΥⲤΤΗΡΙΟΝ ΠΕ ΝΑΛΗΘΕΙΝΟΝ ΟΥⲤΑΡΚΙ
ΚΟΝ ΑΝ ΠΕ ΑΛΛΑ ΕϤΤΒΒΗΥ ΕϤΗΠ` ΑΝ ΑΤΕ
ΠΙΘΥΜΙΑ ΑΛΛΑ ΕΠΟΥΩϢ ΕϤΗΠ` ΑΝ ΕΠΚΑ
ΚΕ Η ΤΟΥϢΗ ΑΛΛΑ ΕϤΗΠ` ΕΠΕϨΟΟΥ ΜΝ
10 ΠΟΥΟΕΙΝ ΟΥΓΑΜΟⲤ ΕϤϢΑΚΩΚ ΑϨΗΥ
ΑϤϢΩΠΕ ΜΠΟΡΝΕΙΑ ΑΥΩ ΤϢΕΛΕΕΤ`
ΟΥ ΜΟΝΟΝ ΕⲤϢΑⲬΙ ΠⲤΠΕΡΜΑ ΝΚΕϨΟ
ΟΥΤ` ΑΛΛΑ ΚΑΝ ΕⲤϢΑΝΡ ΠΒΟΛ` ΜΠΕⲤΚΟΙ
ΤΩΝ ΝⲤΕΝΑΥ ΕΡΟⲤ ΑⲤΠΟΡΝΕΥΕ ΜΟΝΟΝ
15 ΜΑΡΕⲤΟΥΩΝϨ ΕΒΟΛ ΜΠΕⲤΕΙΩΤ` ΜΝ ΤΕⲤ
ΜΑΑΥ ΜΝ ΠϢΒΗΡ ΜΠΝΥΜ`ΦΙΟⲤ ΜΝΝ
ΝϢΗΡΕ ΜΠΝΥΜ`ΦΙΟⲤ ΝΑΕΙ ΕⲤΤΟΕΙ ΝΑΥ
ΕΤΡΟΥΒΩΚ` ΕϨΟΥΝ ΜΜΗΝΕ ΕΠΝΥΜΦΩ
ΝΚΟΟΥΕ ΔΕ ΜΑΡΟῩΡΕΠΙΘΥΜΕΙ ΚΑΝ`

[PAGE 84, PLATE 130]

Even the worldly embrace is a mystery;

far more so, the embrace that incarnates the hidden union.

It is not only a reality of the flesh,

for there is silence in this embrace.

It does not arise from impulse or desire [*epithumia*];

it is an act of will.

It is not of darkness, it is of the light.

If seen by others in the light of day, an ordinary embrace is
 indecent;

if the bride receives the seed of her man outside of their
 bedroom, seen by others, it is indecent.

She may show herself naked only to her father, her mother,
 the friend of her betrothed, and the children of the bridal
 chamber.

These may enter into the bridal chamber;

others cannot hear the voice of the Lover and the Beloved,
 nor breathe their perfume.

20 ЄСѠТM ЄТЄССМН ÑСЄРАПОЛАУЄ M
ПЄССОGÑ АУѠ МАРОУСОNѰ ЄВОЛ ZÑ Ñ
ЛЄЧЛІЧЄ ЄТZЄ ЄВОЛ ZІ ТРАПЄZА ÑѲЄ Ñ
NОУZООР' ОУN ZÑNУМФІОС МÑ ZÑ
NУМФН НП' ЄПNУМФѠN МÑ ОУА NАѰ

25 [N]АУ АПNУМ'ФІОС МÑ ТNУМФН ЄІМН
[NЧѰ].Ѡ.ПЄ MПАЄІ NТЄРЄАВРАZАМ'
[РАѰЄ] ЄТРЄЧNАУ АПЄТЧNАNАУ ЄРОЧ'
[АЧСB]ВЄ ÑТСАРΞ' ÑТАКРОВУСТІА ЄЧТА
[МО M]МОN ХЄ ѰѰЄ ЄТАКО ÑТСАРΞ'

30 [АУѠ МФО].УО. [Ñ]ТЄ [П].КО.С.М.ОС ЄN ZОСОN NОУ
[........ ЄУ].ZН.[П ЄУ].ТѠК. .А.ZЄРАТОУ АУѠ СЄОNZ
[ЄѰХЄ ЄУ].О.УѠN[Z ЄВО].Л. АУМОУ КАТА ППА
[РАΔЄІГМ].А. MПРѠМЄ ЄТОУОNЄZ ЄВОЛ
[ЄN ZОСО].N. MМАZТ' MПРѠМЄ ZНП' ЧОNZ

They can only imagine, like dogs, the crumbs that may fall from
the table.

The embrace of the Lover and the Beloved

belongs to the mystery of the Union;

and only those who have become the same as them can see
them.

123   When Abraham rejoiced in seeing what he was given to see,
he cut the flesh of his foreskin, thus showing us that we
must overcome the limits of the flesh and of the world to
become free.

Certain realities are alive

as long as they are hidden;

when they are made visible, they die.

While people's entrails remain inside them, they are alive.

[PAGE 85, PLATE 131]

ⲚϬⲒ ⲠⲢⲰⲘⲈ ⲈⲨϢⲀϬⲰⲖⲠ' ⲚϬⲒ ⲚⲈϤⲘⲀⲊⲦ
ⲤⲈⲢ̄ ⲠⲂⲞⲖ Ⲛ̄ⲌⲎⲦϤ ϤⲚⲀⲘⲞⲨ ⲚϬⲒ ⲠⲢⲰⲘⲈ
ⲦⲈⲈⲒⲊⲈ ⲞⲚ Ⲙ̄ⲠϢⲎⲚ ⲌⲰⲤ ⲈⲦⲈϤⲚⲞⲨⲚⲈ
ⲌⲎⲠ' ϢⲀϤϯ ⲞⲨⲰ Ⲛ̄ϤⲖⲈⲌⲎⲦ' ⲈⲢϢⲀⲦⲈϤ'
5 ⲚⲞⲨⲚⲈ ϬⲰⲖⲠ' ⲈⲂⲞⲖ ϢⲀⲢⲈⲠϢⲎⲚ ϢⲞ
ⲞⲨⲈ ⲦⲀⲈⲒ ⲦⲈ ⲐⲈ ⲌⲒ ⲬⲠⲞ ⲚⲒⲘ' ⲈⲦⲌⲘ̄ ⲠⲔⲞⲤ
ⲘⲞⲤ ⲞⲨ ⲘⲞⲚⲞⲚ ⲌⲒ ⲚⲈⲦⲞⲨⲞⲚⲌ ⲈⲂⲞⲖ'
ⲀⲖⲖⲀ ⲌⲒ ⲚⲈⲐⲎⲠ' ⲈⲪ ⲌⲞⲤⲞⲚ ⲄⲀⲢ ⲦⲚⲞⲨⲚⲈ
Ⲛ̄ⲦⲔⲀⲔⲒⲀ ⲌⲎⲠ ⲤⲬⲞⲞⲢ ⲈⲨϢⲀⲚⲤⲞⲨⲰⲚⲤ̄
10 ⲆⲈ ⲀⲤⲂⲰⲖ ⲈⲂⲞⲖ ⲈⲤϢⲀⲚⲞⲨⲰⲚⲤ ⲆⲈ Ⲉ
ⲂⲞⲖ ⲀⲤⲰⲬⲚ̄ ⲈⲦⲂⲈ ⲠⲀⲈⲒ ⲠⲖⲞⲄⲞⲤ ⲬⲰ Ⲙ̄
ⲘⲞⲤ ⲬⲈ ⲎⲆⲎ ⲦⲀⲌⲈⲒⲚⲎ Ⲥ̄ⲘⲘⲞⲚⲦ' ⲀⲦⲚⲞⲨ
ⲚⲈ Ⲛ̄Ⲛ̄ϢⲎⲚ ⲈⲤⲚⲀϢⲰⲰⲦ · ⲀⲚ ⲠⲈⲦⲞⲨ
ⲚⲀϢⲀⲀⲦϤ' ⲠⲀⲖⲒⲚ ϢⲀϤϯ ⲞⲨⲰ ⲀⲖⲖⲀ ⲈϢⲀ
15 ⲢⲈⲦⲀⲌⲈⲒⲚⲎ ⲂⲀⲖⲂⲀ̄ ⲈⲠⲒⲦⲚ̄ ⲈⲠⲈⲤⲎⲦ' ϢⲀ
ⲦⲈⲤⲚ̄ ⲦⲚⲞⲨⲚⲈ ⲈⲌⲢⲀⲈⲒ ⲀⲒⲤ̄ ⲆⲈ ⲠⲰⲢⲔ Ⲛ̄
ⲦⲚⲞⲨⲚⲈ Ⲙ̄ⲠⲘⲀ ⲦⲎⲢϤ Ⲍ̄ⲚⲔⲞⲞⲨⲈ ⲆⲈ ⲔⲀ
ⲦⲀ ⲘⲈⲢⲞⲤ ⲀⲚⲞⲚ Ⲍ̄ⲰⲰⲚ' ⲘⲀⲢⲈⲠⲞⲨⲀ
ⲠⲞⲨⲀ Ⲛ̄ⲌⲎⲦⲚ̄ ⲘⲀⲢⲈϤⲂⲀⲖⲂⲖⲈ Ⲛ̄ⲤⲀ ⲦⲚⲞ[Ⲩ]

[PAGE 85, PLATE 131]

If their entrails escape, and are exposed, they die.

It is the same with the tree:

As long as its roots are hidden,

it can grow and flourish; if they are laid open, the tree
   withers.

Thus it is with all that takes birth in the world

of visible and invisible realities.

While the root of evil is hidden, it grows strong;

but if it is disclosed, it is already destroyed.

This is why it is said:

"Already the axe has struck to the root of the trees."[48]

It will not be used to strike at parts that can grow back,

but shall strike deeply at the root, so as to destroy it.

Yeshua uprooted fear, which is the root of evil,

   the poisoner of our lives;

---

48. Cf. Matthew 3:10.

20 ΝΕ ῈΤΚΑΚΙΑ ΕΤῈ2ΡΑῚ Ὲ2ΗΤϤ᾽ ῈϤΠΟΡΚ[Ϲ]

2Α ΤΕϹΝΟΥΝΕ 2Ṁ ΠΕϤ2ΗΤ᾽ ΕϹΝΑΠΩΡΚ

ΔΕ ΕΝ᾽ϢΑϹΟΥΩΝῈ ΕϢΩΠΕ ΔΕ Τῃ

ΝΟ ῈΑΤ᾽ϹΟΟΥΝ ΕΡΟϹ ϹΧΕ ΝΟΥΝΕ 2Ρ[ΑῚ]

Ὲ2ΗΤῃ ΑΥΩ ϹΤΕΥΟ ΕΒΟΛ ῈΝΕϹΚΑΡ

25 ΠΟϹ 2ΡΑῚ 2Ṁ Πῃ2ΗΤ᾽ ϹΟ ῈΧΟΕΙϹ ΕΡῸ

ΤῃΝΟ ῈϨΜ͞Ϩ͞ᾼΛͅ ΝΑϹ Ϲ͞ΡΑΙΧΜΑΛ[ΩΤΙ]ͅΖ̣ͅ[Ε]

Ṁ͞ΜΟΝ ΕΤΡῈΕΙΡΕ ῈΝΕΤῈΟΥΟ[Ϣ ΟΥ ΑΝ]

ΝΕΤῈΟΥΟϢΟΥ ΤῈΕΙΡΕ Ṁ͞ΜΟΟΥ [ΑΝ Ϲ]

Ϭ͞ΜϬΟΜ ΧΕ Ṁ͞ΠῈ͞ϹΟΥΩΝῈ 2ΩϹ [ΕϹϢΟ]

30 ΟΠ ΜΕΝ Ϲ͞ΡΕΝΕΡΓΕΙ Τͅ.Μ͞.ῈΤΑΤ.Ϲ.[ΟΟΥΝ]

ΕϹϢΟΟΠ Ṁ͞ΜΑΑΥ ῈΝΠΕ[ΘΟΟΥ ΝΟΝ]

ΤΜ͞ῈΤΑΤ᾽ϹΟΟΥΝ [Ϣ]ͅΜ.ϢΕ Α[ΠΜΟΥ]

ΝΕΤ᾽ϢΟΟΠ᾽ ΕΒΟΛ ͅ2Ν͞ͅ ΤΜῈ[ΤΑΤϹΟΟΥΝ]

ΟΥΤΕ ΝΕΥϢΟΟΠ ΑΝ᾽ ΟΥΤ[Ε ϹΕϢΟΟΠ ΑΝ]

35 ΟΥΤΕ ϹΕΝΑϢΩΠΕ ᾼΝ.ͅ [ΝΕΤ2Ν ΤΜΕ ΔΕ]

but he only uprooted a part of it,

leaving it to us to dig out our own roots,

so that each person works to uproot from their own heart

that evil which is the cause of unhappiness.

We uproot it if we recognize it,

but if we do not want to recognize

that which is wrong in us, how can we uproot it?

This bad root bears its fruits in us and in this world;

it will dominate us, and make us its slaves,

so that we do what we do not want to do

and are no longer able to do what we want to do.

Its power is our ignorance or refusal to know it.

As long as it is there, it is working:

Ignorance is the cause of all evil, and serves death.

Nothing has been or ever will be born from ignorance.

Those who live in vigilance will be happy

when the truth is revealed.

[PAGE 86, PLATE 132]

ⲤⲈⲚⲀⲬⲰⲔ ⲈⲂⲞⲗ ⲌⲞⲦⲀⲚ ⲈⲢⲮⲀⲦⲀⲗⲎⲐⲈⲒⲀ
ⲦⲎⲢⲤ ⲞⲨⲰⲚⲌ ⲈⲂⲞⲗ ⲦⲀⲗⲎⲐⲈⲒⲀ ⲄⲀⲢ ⲔⲀⲦⲀ ⲐⲈ
Ⲛ̄ⲦⲘⲚ̄ⲦⲀⲦ’ⲤⲞⲞⲨⲚ ⲈⲤⲌⲎⲠ’ ⲘⲈⲚ Ⲥ̄ⲢⲀⲚⲀ
ⲠⲀⲨⲈ ⲌⲢⲀⲒ̈ Ⲛ̄ⲌⲎⲦⲤ̄ ⲈⲤⲮⲀⲞⲨⲰⲚⲌ ⲆⲈ ⲈⲂⲞⲗ
5 Ⲛ̄ⲤⲈⲤⲞⲨⲰⲚⲤ̄ ⲮⲀⲨⲦ ⲚⲀⲤ ⲈⲞⲞⲨ ⲌⲞⲤⲞⲚ
ⲤⲄ̄Ⲛ̄ⲄⲞⲘ ⲈⲦⲘⲚ̄ⲦⲀⲦⲤⲞⲞⲨⲚ ⲀⲨⲰ ⲀⲦ’ⲠⲖⲀ
ⲚⲎ Ⲥ†̄ Ⲛ̄ⲦⲘⲚ̄ⲦⲈⲗⲈⲨⲐⲈⲢⲞⲤ ⲠⲈⲬⲀⲨ Ⲛ̄ⲄⲒ
ⲠⲖⲞⲄⲞⲤ ⲬⲈ ⲈⲦⲈⲦⲚ̄ⲮⲀⲚⲤⲞⲨⲰⲚ ⲦⲀⲗⲎ
ⲐⲈⲒⲀ ⲦⲀⲗⲎⲐⲈⲒⲀ ⲚⲀⲢ̄ ⲦⲎⲚⲈ Ⲛ̄ⲈⲗⲈⲨⲐⲈⲢⲞⲤ
10 ⲦⲘⲚ̄ⲦⲀⲦⲤⲞⲞⲨⲚ’ ⲤⲞ Ⲛ̄ⲌⲘⲌⲀ̄ⲗ̄ ⲦⲄⲚⲰⲤⲒⲤ ⲞⲨ
ⲈⲗⲈⲨⲐⲈⲢⲒⲀ ⲦⲈ ⲈⲚⲮⲀⲤⲞⲨⲰⲚ ⲦⲀⲗⲎⲐⲈⲒⲀ
Ⲧ̄ⲚⲀⲤⲈ ⲀⲚⲔⲀⲢⲠⲞⲤ Ⲛ̄ⲦⲀⲗⲎⲐⲈⲒⲀ ⲌⲢⲀⲒ̈ Ⲛ̄
ⲌⲎⲦⲚ̄ ⲈⲚⲮⲀⲌⲰⲦⲢ̄ ⲈⲢⲞⲤ ⲤⲚⲀⲬⲒ Ⲙ̄ⲠⲚ̄ⲠⲖⲎ
ⲢⲰⲘⲀ ⲦⲈⲚⲞⲨ ⲞⲨⲚ̄ⲦⲀⲚ’ Ⲙ̄ⲘⲀⲨ Ⲛ̄ⲚⲈⲦⲞⲨ
15 ⲞⲚⲌ ⲈⲂⲞⲗ · Ⲛ̄ⲦⲈ ⲠⲤⲰⲚⲦ’ ⲮⲀⲚⲬⲞⲞⲤ ⲬⲈ
Ⲛ̄ⲦⲞⲞⲨ ⲚⲈ Ⲛ̄ⲬⲰⲰⲢⲈ ⲈⲦ’ⲦⲀⲈⲒⲎⲨ ⲚⲈⲐⲎⲠ’
ⲆⲈ ⲚⲈ ⲚⲄⲰⲂ’ ⲈⲦⲮⲎⲤ ⲦⲀⲈⲒ ⲦⲈ ⲐⲈ Ⲛ̄ⲚⲈⲦⲞⲨ
ⲞⲚⲌ ⲈⲂⲞⲗ’ Ⲛ̄ⲦⲀⲗⲎⲐⲈⲒⲀ ⲌⲚ̄ⲄⲰⲂ’ ⲚⲈ ⲀⲨⲰ
ⲤⲈⲮⲎⲤ ⲚⲈⲐⲎⲠ’ ⲆⲈ Ⲛ̄ⲬⲰⲢⲈ ⲚⲈ ⲀⲨⲰ ⲤⲈⲦⲀ

[PAGE 86, PLATE 132]

While hidden, truth is like ignorance:

It keeps to itself.

But when it is revealed, it is recognized and glorified,

for it is more powerful than ignorance and error.

It brings freedom.

The *Logos* said: "If you know the truth, the truth shall make
you free."[49]

Ignorance is slavery,

knowledge [*gnosis*] is freedom.

When we recognize the truth, we taste its fruits in ourselves.

When we unite with truth, it shares its fullness [*pleroma*] with
us.

124 We know what creation reveals to us,

and call these things strong and worthy;

that which is unknown to us we deem weak and
contemptible.

So it is that the realities revealed to vigilance seem weak and
contemptible,

whereas they are strong and praiseworthy.

---

49. Cf. John 8:32.

20 ЄІНУ СЄОУОΝ2 ΔЄ ЄΒΟΛ Ν̄6Ι Μ̄ΜΥΣΤΗΡῙΟ
Ν̄ΤΑΛΗΘЄΙΑ ЄΥΟ Ν̄ΤΥΠΟΣ 2Ι 2ΙΚΩΝ ΠΚΟΙ
ΤΩΝ ΔЄ Ч2ΗΠ' Ν̄ΤΟЧ ΠЄ ΠЄΤΟΥΑΑΒ' 2Μ̄
ΠЄΤΟΥΑΑΒ ΝЄΡЄΠΚΑΤΑΠЄΤΑΣΜΑ ΜЄΝ ·
2ΟΒϹ̄ Ν̄ϢΟΡΠ · ΠΩΣ ЄΡЄΠΝΟΥΤЄ Ρ̄ΔΙΟΙΚЄΙ
25 Ν̄ΤΚΤΙΣΙΣ ЄЧϢΑΠΩΣ ΔЄ Ν̄6Ι ΠΚΑΤΑΠЄ
.ΤΑϹ.[ΜΑ] ΑΥΩ Ν̄ΤЄΝΑ ΠϹΑ Ν2ΟΥΝ' ΟΥΩΝ2
[ЄΒΟΛ] ϹЄΝΑΚΩ ΔЄ Μ̄ΠЄЄΙΗЄΙ Ν̄ϹΩΟΥ
[ЄЧΟ] .Ν.ЄΡΗΜΟΣ ΜΑΛΛΟΝ ΔЄ ϹЄΝΑΡ̄ΚΑΤΑ
[ΛΥЄ Μ̄]ΜΟЧ' ΤΜ̄Ν̄ΤΝΟΥΤЄ ΔЄ ΤΗΡϹ ϹΑΠΩΤ
30 [ЄΒΟΛ 2]Ν̄ ΝЄЄΙΜΑ Є2ΟΥΝ ΑΝ ЄΝЄΤΟΥΑΑΒ
[Ν̄ΝЄΤΟ]ΥΑΑΒ ϹΝΑϢ ΤΩϹ ΓΑΡ ΑΝ ΜΝ̄ ΠΟΥ
[ΟЄΙΝ Ν̄ΑΤ]'ΤΩ2 Μ[Ν̄] ΠΠΛΗΡΩΜΑ Ν̄ΑΤ`
[ϢΤΑ ΑΛΛ]Α ϹΝ.Α.[ϢΩ]ΠЄ 2Α Ν̄ΤΝ2 Μ̄ΠϹϤΟϹ
[ΑΥΩ 2Α ΝЄ]Ч6ΒΟЄΙ ΤЄЄΙ6ΙΒΩΤΟϹ ΝΑϢΩ
35 [ΠЄ ΝΑϹ Ν̄Ο].Υ.ΟΥΧΑЄΙ Ν̄ΤΑΡЄΠΚΑΤΑΚΛΥϹ

The mysteries of Truth are manifested to us

in the form of archetypes or images.

125 The bridal chamber, where Union is realized, is hidden from

us; it is the holy of holies.

The veil conceals what we cannot see:

the way in which God informs creation.

When the veil is torn and the inner is made manifest,

we will abandon our house of desolation, and it will be

destroyed.

But divinity, in its fullness, will not desert these places, so as

to dwell only in the holy of holies;

it will not want to merge immediately into the unmixed

light, the fullness that knows no lack;

it will go under the arms and wings of the cross.

This ark will be our refuge when the waters come.

[PAGE 87, PLATE 133]

ΜΟϹ ⲘⲘΟΟⲨ ΕΜΑⲌⲦΕ ΕⲌΡΑϊ ΕⲬϪΟⲨ ΕΡⲰΑ

ⲌⲚ̄ⲌΟΕΙΝΕ ⲰⲰⲠΕ ⲌⲚ̄ ⲦⲪⲨⲀⲎ Ⲛ̄ⲦⲘⲚ̄ⲦΟⲨ

ⲎⲎⲂ ΝΑΕΙ Ⲛ̄ΑⲰ Ϭⲛ̄Ϭ ⲞⲘ̄ Ⲛ̄ⲂⲰⲔ̓ ΕⲌΟⲨΝ Ε

ⲠϹⲀ ⲚⲌ ΟⲨΝ Ⲙ̄ⲠⲔⲀⲦⲀⲠΕⲦⲀϹⲘΑ ⲘⲚ̄ ⲠⲀⲢ

5 ⲬΙΕΡΕⲨϹ ΕⲦⲂΕ ⲠⲀΕΙ Ⲙ̄ⲠΕⲠⲔⲀⲦⲀⲠΕⲦⲀϹ

ⲘⲀ ⲠⲰϹ Ⲙ̄ⲠϹⲀ Ⲛ̄ⲦⲠΕ ΟⲨⲀⲀⲦϤ̄ ΕⲠΕΙ ΝΕⲨ

ΝⲀΟⲨΕΝ Ⲛ̄ΝⲀ ⲠϹⲀ ⲚⲦⲠΕ ΟⲨⲀⲀⲦΟⲨ · ΟⲨⲦΕ

Ⲙ̄ⲠϹⲀ Ⲙ̄ⲠⲒⲦⲚ̄ ΟⲨⲀⲀⲦϤ̓ ΑΝ Ⲛ̄ⲦⲀϤⲠⲰϹ ΕⲠΕΙ

ΝⲀϤΝⲀΟⲨⲰⲚⲌ ΕⲂΟⲀ Ⲛ̄ΝⲀ ⲠϹⲀ Ⲙ̄ⲠⲒⲦⲚ̄ ΟⲨ

10 ⲀⲀⲨ ⲀⲀⲀⲀ Ⲛ̄ⲦⲀϤⲠⲰϹ Ⲛ̄ⲦⲠΕ ΕⲠⲒⲦⲚ̄ ΑΝⲀ

ⲠϹⲀ ⲚⲦⲠΕ ΟⲨⲰⲚ̓ ΝⲀΝ Ⲛ̄ΝΕⲦⲘ̄ⲠϹⲀ Ⲙ̄ⲠⲒ

ⲦⲚ̄ ϪΕⲔⲀⲀϹ ΕΝΝⲀⲂⲰⲔ̓ ΕⲌΟⲨΝ̓ ⲀⲠⲠΕⲐⲎⲠ̓

Ⲛ̄ⲦⲀⲀⲎⲐΕΙⲀ ⲠⲀΕΙ ⲀⲀⲎⲐⲰϹ ⲠΕ ⲠΕⲦ̓ⲦⲀΕΙ

ⲎⲨ ΕⲦΟ Ⲛ̄ⲬⲰⲰΡΕ ΕΝⲀⲂⲰⲔ ⲆΕ ΕⲌΟⲨΝ ΕΜⲀⲨ

15 ⲌⲒⲦⲚ̄ ⲌⲚ̄ⲦⲨⲠΟϹ ΕⲨⲰⲎϹ ⲘⲚ̄ ⲌⲚ̄ⲘⲚ̄ⲦϬⲰⲂ

ϹΕⲰⲎϹ ΜΕΝ̓ Ⲛ̄ΝⲀⲌΡⲚ̄ ⲠΕΟΟⲨ ΕⲦϪⲎⲔ̓ ΕⲂΟ[Ⲁ]

ΟⲨⲚ̄ ΕΟΟⲨ ΕϤϪΟϹΕ ΕΟΟⲨ ΟⲨⲚ̄ Ϭ ΟⲘ̓ ΕϤϪ.Ο.

ϹΕ ΕϬΟⲘ̓ ΕⲦⲂΕ ⲠⲀΕΙ ⲀΝ̓ⲦΕⲀΕΙΟΝ̓ ΟⲨΕΝ

ΝⲀΝ ⲘⲚ̄ ΝΕⲐⲎⲠ̓ Ⲛ̄ⲦⲀⲀⲎⲐΕΙⲀ ⲀⲨⲰ ΝΕⲦΟ[Ⲩ]

[PAGE 87, PLATE 133]

If there are priests, they shall be allowed to go into the interior,
    beyond the veil, along with the high priest.
This is why the veil is not only torn above,
and not only torn below,
but torn from above to below;
that which is above
opens itself to us who are below,
so that we, too, enter the secret of the truth.
It is through fragile images and symbols
that we penetrate into that which is worthy of reverence and
    filled with power.
These relative realties are indeed trivial before the Absolute.
Glory beyond glory, power beyond power;
fullness is offered to us in the secret of vigilance;
the holy of holies is made manifest;
and through the sacred embrace, we are invited into the interior.

20 ААВ ῈΝΕΤΟΥΑΑΒ ΑΥ6ΩΛΠˈ ΕΒΟΛˈ ΑΥΩ Α
ΠΚΟΙΤΩΝ ΤΩ2Μ ΜΜΟΝ Ε2ΟΥΝˈ ΕΝ 2ΟΟ̄
ΜΕΝˈ Υ2ΗΠˈ ΤΚΑΚΙΑ ΟΥΟΟΥ ΜΕΝ ΜΠΟΥ
ΥΙΤ̄2 ΔΕ ῈΤΜΗΤΕ ΜΠΟΠΕΡΜΑ ΜΠΠῈ[Ᾱ]
ΕΤΟΥΑΑΒˈ ΟΕΟ Ὲ2Μ2ᾹᾹ ῈΤΠΟΝΗΡΙΑ 2Ο

25 ΤΑΝ ΔΕ ΕΥΨΑ6ΩΛΠˈ ΕΒΟΛ ΤΟΤΕ ΠΟΥΟ
ΕΙΝ ῈΤΕΛΕΙΟΝˈ ΝΑ2ΑΤΕ ΕΒΟΛˈ ΕΧ[Ν Ο]Υ.Ο.[Ν]
ΝΙΜ · ΑΥΩ ΝΕΤῈ2ΗΤΥˈ ΤΗΡΟΥ ΟΕ.Ν.[ΑΧΙ ΠΧΡΙ]
ΟΜΑ ΤΟΤΕ Ὲ2Μ2ᾹᾹ ῈΑΡ̄ ΕΛΕΥΘΕ[ΡΟΟ ΑΥΩ]
ῈΟΕΟΩΤΕ ῈΑΙΧΜΑΛΩΤΟΟ ΤΩ6Ε [ΝΙΜ ΕΜ]

30 ΠΕ ΠΑΕΙΩΤ ˈ ΕΤ2Ῡ ΜΠΗΥΕ ΤΟ6Υ [ΟΕΝΑ]
ΠΟΡΚΥˈ ΝΕΤΠΟΡΧˈ ΟΕΝΑ2ΩΤ[Ρ̄ Μ]Μ[ΟΟΥ ΑΥΩ]
ΟΕΝΑΜΟΥ2 ΟΥΟ.Ν. .ΝΙΜ.ˈ Ε.Τ.Ν[ΑΒΩΚ Ε2ΟΥΝ]
ΕΠΚΟΙΤΩΝ ΟΕΝΑ.ΧΕΡ.Ο ΜΠ.Ο.[ΥΟΕΙΝ ΜΕΥΧΠ]
Ο ΓΑΡ ῈΘΕ ῈῙΓΑΜΟΟ ΕΤῈΝ[ΑΥ ΕΡΟΟΥ ΑΝ ΕΥ]

35 ΨΩΠΕ ῈΤΟΥΨΗ ΠΚΩΟΤˈ .Ψ.[ΑΥΜΟΥ2]

As long as this is hidden, unhappiness prevails;

it always poisons the seeds [*sperma*], and evil is at work.

But when it is manifest,

the clear light will envelop all, and everyone

who finds themselves in it will be anointed [*khrisma*].

Slaves and prisoners will be freed.

126   If a plant has not been planted by my Father who is in heaven,
it will be uprooted.[50]

Those who were separated will reunite and become fertilized.

All those who practice the sacred embrace [*koiton*] will kindle
the light;

they will not beget as people do

in ordinary marriages, which take place in darkness.

---

50. Cf. Matthew 15:13.

[PAGE 88, PLATE 134]

ⲚⲦⲞⲨϢⲎ ϢⲀϤⲬⲈⲚⲈ ⲘⲘⲨⲤⲦⲎⲢⲒⲞⲚ ⲆⲈ
ⲘⲠⲒⲄⲀⲘⲞⲤ ⲚⲦⲞϤ ϢⲀⲨⲬⲰⲔ' ⲈⲂⲞⲖ' ⲌⲘ ⲠⲈ
ⲌⲞⲞⲨ' ⲘⲚ ⲠⲞⲨⲞⲈⲒⲚ ⲘⲀⲢⲈϤⲪⲞⲞⲨ ⲈⲦⲘⲘⲀⲨ
Ⲏ ⲠⲈϤⲞⲨⲞⲈⲒⲚ ⲌⲰⲦⲠ ⲈⲢϢⲀⲞⲨⲀ ϢⲰⲠⲈ Ⲛ
5 ϢⲎⲢⲈ ⲘⲠⲚⲨⲘⲪⲰⲚ' ϤⲚⲀϪⲒ ⲘⲠⲞⲨⲞⲈⲒⲚ
ⲈⲦⲘⲞⲨⲀ ϪⲒⲦϤ ⲈϤⲚ̄ⲚⲈⲈⲒⲘⲀ ϤⲚⲀϢ ϪⲒⲦϤ'
ⲀⲚ ⲘⲠⲔⲈⲘⲀ ⲠⲈⲦⲀϪⲒ ⲠⲞⲨⲞⲈⲒⲚ ⲈⲦⲘⲘⲀⲨ
ⲤⲈⲚⲀⲚⲀⲨ ⲀⲚ · ⲈⲢⲞϤ ⲞⲨⲦⲈ ⲤⲈⲚⲀϢ ⲈⲘⲀⲌⲦⲈ
ⲀⲚ' ⲘⲘⲞϤ ⲀⲨⲰ ⲘⲚ ⲖⲀⲀⲨ ⲚⲀϢ ⲢⲤⲔⲨⲖⲖⲈ Ⲙ
10 ⲠⲀⲈⲒ ⲚⲦⲈⲈⲒⲘⲈⲒⲚⲈ ⲔⲀⲚ ⲈϤⲢⲠⲞⲖⲒⲦⲈⲨⲈⲤ
ⲐⲀⲒ ⲌⲘ ⲠⲔⲞⲤⲘⲞⲤ ⲀⲨⲰ ⲞⲚ ⲈϤϢⲀⲈⲒ ⲈⲂⲞⲖ
ⲌⲘ ⲠⲔⲞⲤⲘⲞⲤ ⲎⲆⲎ ⲀϤϪⲒ ⲚⲦⲀⲖⲎⲐⲈⲒⲀ ⲌⲚ
Ⲛ̄ⲤⲒⲔⲰⲚ ⲠⲔⲞⲤⲘⲞⲤ ⲀϤϢⲰⲠⲈ Ⲛ̄ⲚⲀⲒⲰ
ⲠⲀⲒⲰⲚ ⲄⲀⲢ ⲈϤϢⲞⲞⲠ' ⲚⲀϤ ⲘⲠⲖⲎⲢⲰ
15 ⲘⲀ ⲀⲨⲰ ⲈϤϢⲞⲞⲠ' ⲚⲦⲈⲈⲒⲤⲈ ϤⲞⲨⲞⲚⲌ ⲈⲂⲞⲖ
ⲚⲀϤ ⲞⲨⲀⲀϤ ⲈϤⲌⲎⲠ' ⲀⲚ ⲌⲘ ⲠⲔⲀⲔⲈ ⲘⲚ ⲦⲞⲨ
ϢⲎ ⲀⲖⲖⲀ ⲈϤⲌⲎⲠ ⲌⲚ̄Ⲛ ⲞⲨⲌⲞⲞⲨ ⲚⲦⲈⲖⲈⲒⲞ̄
ⲘⲚ ⲞⲨⲞⲈⲒⲚ ⲈϤⲞⲨⲀⲀⲂ ⲠⲈⲨⲀⲄⲄⲈⲖⲒⲞ̄Ⲛ
ⲠⲔ̄Ⲁ̄Ⲧ̄Ⲁ̄ Ⲫ̄Ⲓ̄Ⲗ̄Ⲓ̄Ⲡ̄Ⲡ̄Ⲟ̄Ⲥ̄

[PAGE 88, PLATE 134]

The fire that burns by night flares up, and then is gone;

but the mystery of that embrace is never extinguished;

it happens in that light of day which knows no sunset.

127   If someone experiences Trust and Consciousness in the heart
     of the embrace,

they become a child of light.

If someone does not receive these,

it is because they remain attached to what they know;

when they cease to be attached, they will be able to receive
     them.

Whoever receives this light in nakedness will no longer be
     recognizable;

none will be able to grasp them, none will be able to make
     them sad or miserable,

whether they are in this world, or have left it.

They already know the truth in images.

For them, this world has become another world,

and this Temple Space [*Aeon*] is fullness [*pleroma*].

They are who they are. They are one.

Neither shadow nor night can hide them.

BOOKS OF RELATED INTEREST

The Gospel of Mary Magdalene
by Jean-Yves Leloup

The Gospel of John in the Light of Indian Mysticism
by Ravi Ravindra

Gnostic Secrets of the Naassenes
The Initiatory Teachings of the Last Supper
by Mark H. Gaffney

The Way of the Essenes
Christ's Hidden Life Remembered
by Anne and Daniel Meurois-Givaudan

The Woman with the Alabaster Jar
Mary Magdalen and the Holy Grail
by Margaret Starbird

Magdalene's Lost Legacy
Symbolic Numbers and the Sacred Union in Christianity
by Margaret Starbird

The Church of Mary Magdalene
The Sacred Feminine and the Treasure of Rennes-Le-Château
by Jean Markale

Cathedral of the Black Madonna
The Druids and the Mysteries of Chartres
by Jean Markale

Inner Traditions • Bear & Company
P.O. Box 388
Rochester, VT 05767
1-800-246-8648
www.InnerTraditions.com

Or contact your local bookseller